My Amalfi Coast Love Affair

by

Margie Miklas

My Amalfi Coast Love Affair
Copyright © 2018 Margie Miklas

Edited by Susan Hughes

Cover Design: La Maison Publishing, Inc.
Cover Photo by Margie Miklas
Published by Margie Miklas

Please visit my blog, Margie in Italy, to see my original photos from many of the places mentioned in this book. https://margieinitaly.com

Dedicated to Richard,

who elevated my love affair with the Amalfi Coast

to a whole new level.

"Margie is the everywoman of us in the sense that we've all been that girl wishing we packed less and practiced more on the stair-master before tackling Amalfi's perilous staircases. Her love affair with one of Italy's most glittery coastlines is as palpable and relatable as it gets and I would absolutely recommend this book for anyone who appreciates an honest, human approach to a popular place." —Georgette Jupe-Pradier, Editor of *Italy Magazine* and creator of the popular *Girl in Florence* blog

"Margie has both great knowledge and great passion for her subject, bella Italia. She's the perfect host to guide you around the often confusing--but always alluring--Amalfi Coast. Go along with her on this adventure and you, too, will fall hopelessly in love with this idyllic corner of Italy. Buon viaggio! —Rick Zullo, Blogger at Rick's Rome and podcaster at The Fatal Charm of Italy

"Margie's intimate and heartwarming love for the Amalfi Coast becomes enriched and transformed when, after numerous visits with family, friends, and even solo... she shares it with the love of her life. What a perfect happy ending to a dual love affair!" —Victoria De Maio, Author of Victoria's Travel TipZ Italian Style: MORE Simple Ways to Enjoy Italian Ways on Your Next Trip to Italy

"Margie's ability to take readers on a journey with her is special. Her willingness to open her heart and allow us to share in her experiences is unique. It is like reading her diary, a travel guide and a delightful novel at the same time. You can truly feel her 'Love Affair' with the Amalfi Coast in this book." —Jennifer Spitalieri, Editor of La Gazzetta Italiana

"Having lived in Positano for almost 20 years, although I never take for granted the beauty of the area, I suppose I have forgotten what it is like to see it and explore the streets for the first few times as a returning visitor. *My Amalfi Coast Love Affair* vividly describes the feelings one experiences when seeing Positano and the Amalfi Coast for the first time. Margie spends her time here well, meeting various residents and taking day trips around the area to see as much as she possibly can. If you need an Italy fix or just want to be spirited away to the Amalfi Coast for a while, then this book is for you." —Nicki Positano, Social Media Influencer *@NickiPositano*

"Clinging to the cliff-sides south of Naples, the villages of the Amalfi Coast are so picturesque and unique that UNESCO has recognized them with a special designation. Margie Miklas takes us on a personal journey around this beautiful Italian peninsula, sharing her stories and meanderings. A memoir as colorful as the Amalfi Coast itself." —Laura Morelli, Ph.D., Art Historian and Historical Novelist.

I don't know what it is about the Amalfi Coast that tugs at my heart and makes me wish I was there, more than any other place in Italy. I think it must be a combination of things that draws me to this coastline in southern Italy. It's no secret to those who know me that I love being near the water. My home is in Florida, and in ten minutes I can be on Indian River Drive, a scenic roadway adjacent to the intracoastal waterway, which is only separated from the Atlantic Ocean by a narrow strip of land known as Hutchinson Island. The drive is pretty and serene, a perfect antidote and escape from the stress of a busy life.

So naturally, I find peace and solace along the Amalfi Coast, especially whenever I stare at the azure water of the Tyrrhenian Sea. This sea can be calm and quiet, or it can be angry and loud. October is the time for the sirocco, a warm, humid wind which originates over the Sahara Desert in North Africa as a dry wind. As it crosses the Mediterranean toward southern Italy, it picks up moisture.

But it's more than being near the sea that beckons me back to the Amalfi Coast. The individual little towns that sprout up from the rugged landscape and steep rocky cliffs present their own appeal and special sense of character for me. Tiered, colorful communes which were once simple fishing villages fascinate me with their miniature shops and trattorias.

I like how almost all the businesses are independent, family-run enterprises, sometimes for generations. These local entrepreneurs feel a sense of pride in what they do, and they love to share the experience with anyone who shows an interest.

The sheer beauty, the rocky precipices, the tantalizing location on the sea, and the people entice me to the Amalfi

Coast year after year. But there is still more to this allure. Life here seems simple, and yet, at the same time, it is difficult. By geography and topography alone, most Amalfi Coast towns are built into hills and cliffs. This fact necessitates narrow winding roads cut out of the rock and, in some instances, steep staircases to navigate through the towns.

In Positano, in order to reach my hotel on Fornillo Beach, a minimum of three hundred stairs from the parking area on Viale Pasitea is the only option available. The road for cars ends, and walking down to the beach is the only way to arrive, unless you are coming by ferry or boat. I marvel at the fortitude of the local residents as they climb up and down these steps with ease as part of their daily routine. As a traveler, I am grateful for the muscular young men like Adriano who work as porters. They carry the luggage either on carts or on their backs, and they do it with a smile.

Not to be overlooked, the food is a huge part of the attraction of the Amalfi Coast, especially its simplicity. Always fresh, the seafood is plentiful and most likely comes from the day's catch by the locals who make fishing their livelihood. The fruits and vegetables are abundant, grown on the terraced land high above the sea. Lemon groves flourish and tomatoes, fennel, basil, and arugula are in season much of the year due to the moderate Mediterranean climate.

When I spend time on the Amalfi Coast, I am invigorated, inspired, and happy. A peacefulness envelops me, and I see this place as a paradise.

By relating my experiences, I'll try to impart a sense of my love affair with the Amalfi Coast to you. I hope you'll feel like you're there with me as I share my stories, in no particular order, with you.

Buon viaggio.

Table of Contents

Traveling to the Amalfi Coast – It's a Process

As famous and beautiful as the Amalfi Coast is, no easy way exists to reach this coastal, rocky location in southern Italy. Maybe that's why it's not one of the places first-time Italy travelers place on their itinerary.

The year is 2007, and it's my first time in Italy. I'm traveling with my brother Rick and sister-in-law Monica, both of whom have been to Italy before. But this journey to the celebrated Amalfi Coast is a first for all of us. After spending a busy week in Rome, I'm more than ready for some tranquility and relaxation farther south.

Our plan to take a taxi from our Rome apartment to Roma Termini, the main train station, suddenly changes—and not by choice. I am informed by a taxi driver that the taxis are *in sciopero* (on strike). I understand that strikes are part of the Italian lifestyle and a common occurrence, especially in the transportation sector. These work stoppages are usually staged as a form of protest against the laws or politics of the day and can last anywhere from four to twenty-four hours. They are often scheduled in advance, so the locals can plan alternative travel arrangements. Unfortunately, this is all new for tourists like me, and it requires flexibility and a change in plans. I'm learning that in Italy, situations can change at a moment's notice.

So for the three of us, our substitute plan consists of taking the metro, or subway. With our luggage in tow, we trudge through the rain, heading up Via del Corso to the metro station five blocks away. "This sucks," Monica says. "How much farther is it?" Even Rick, who loves to get as much exercise as possible, isn't amused by the unplanned walk in the rain, as he dodges the throngs of pedestrians walking on the narrow sidewalk.

One of Rome's main thoroughfares, the Corso, or as locals say, "il Corso," begins at Piazza del Popolo in the north and runs in a straight line to Piazza Venezia, where the gigantic Vittorio Emanuele II monument can't be missed. Always crowded, both with automobiles and pedestrians, il Corso follows the track of ancient Rome's Via Lata, and at one time was a venue for horse races. Monica is not a fan after falling earlier this week in an attempt to avert running into another pedestrian. "If I never have to see il Corso again I'll be happy," she says. "This street is crazy."

After a ten-minute walk, which seems even longer in this inclement weather, Rick, Monica, and I arrive at the Spagna metro station, located on a side street near Piazza di Spagna, at the bottom of the always-busy Spanish Steps. Drenched, cold, and tired, we make our way to the underground platform. The escalator, combined with the multitude of steps inside the station, is a brutal reality check that large suitcases do not make sense for European travel. *Why did I bring this damn huge suitcase with me? Note to self: next time pack light.* I am positive the locals find us amusing, as we must stand out as typical American tourists. The steep staircases in Rome's metro station make traveling with heavy luggage an exasperating task. I'm cursing under my breath with each step.

Since we are traveling in the morning, I anticipate the metro to be packed with commuters, but once our train arrives at the platform, I'm relieved to discover that it isn't completely full. The three of us board, overstuffed bags and all, and I'm happy to be on our way. None of us complain that we are forced to stand, as the ride to the Termini train station is only three stops away.

Once there, we realize we are early for our scheduled Trenitalia departure to Naples. But better to be early than late, I'm thinking. "I'm hungry. I see a place where we can sit down and have a little breakfast," I say. Breakfast at a train station is surprisingly good, especially when a *cornetto* and a beverage is all we want. Rick grabs a piece of fruit to stay true to his healthy eating—except for the mandatory Coca Cola Light. Monica is the only one who orders coffee. Having time to savor the taste of Italian pastries in a warm place is another reason I'm grateful. I especially like the *cornetto al cioccolato*, filled with delicious Nutella.

After we finish eating, we check the massive train schedule board overhead, which lists the upcoming departures and arrivals. To our dismay our train is *retardo* (delayed). Originally scheduled to depart at 12:45 p.m., the new time is listed for 1:20 p.m., but the good news is the train is already on the *binario* (track). We locate our carriage, #10, and find our assigned seats. After the stressful walk this morning, this Eurostar train is luxurious. Our bags fit conveniently in the luggage area, and our seats are comfortable.

Trains in Europe generally run on time, but not always, and this one finally pulls out of the station at 1:33 p.m. One hundred forty-four miles and an hour and twenty minutes later, we arrive at Napoli Centrale, the main station in Naples. The real highlight of this scenic journey is a view of the larger-than-life Vesuvius volcano, a decidedly different change of scenery after miles of rolling hills with grazing sheep. On the approach to Naples, though, the landscape deteriorates as the train glides by the slum-like apartment houses and graffiti-laced stations. Not a great PR pitch for this old city in the south of Italy. On to the next leg of today's trip.

Today is my first visit to the Amalfi Coast. This thirty-three-mile stretch of rugged winding coastline in southern Italy is not such an easy destination to reach. No trains or airports service this place in the Campania region of Italy, and the available travel options consist of buses, ferries, and private driver services.

Even though three of us are traveling together, our budget doesn't allow for the costly option of a private driver. So, today's transportation of choice becomes the regional narrow-gauge train known as the Circumvesuviana. This is basically a commuter train which local residents use to get to and from their jobs for an affordable fare. The train line is aptly named because its twenty-nine-mile itinerary connects the city of Naples with no less than thirty individual towns around Mount Vesuvius before it reaches its final destination of Sorrento; hence, *circum* (around) and *Vesuviana* (Vesuvius). Although Sorrento is not actually part of the Amalfi Coast, it is a lovely city which serves as an excellent hub and gateway to the Amalfi Coast.

As an inexperienced international traveler, I am toting a huge suitcase which weighs fifty pounds, the maximum allowed for overseas travel. To purchase tickets for the train to Sorrento, we have to walk through the main Naples train station and go downstairs to the underground Garibaldi station, which is the station for the Circumvesuviana train. Just like in the Rome metro, the luggage quickly becomes even more of an aggravation for train travel, as I have to drag it up and down countless steps just to reach the secondary station. *This is crazy. Whoever heard of a train station inside a train station? What a pain. Aren't there any elevators?* At the nondescript ticket booth, we purchase one-way tickets for €3.20 apiece, cash only. The whole operation seems circumspect and old-fashioned to me, but it's the only way we are going to get to Sorrento, so we do what we need to do.

I'm told this train is almost always crowded and dirty, so my expectations are not high, and I assume I'll have to stand during the one-hour journey from Naples to Sorrento. According to my research of current travel guides, these trains are rife with pickpockets, and I am somewhat nervous, but I tell myself the trip is a little safer since I'm not traveling alone.

While waiting on the platform, I notice that quite a few of the other passengers are smoking, and the entire area has an unpleasant smell. After some time, the train arrives and, true to its reputation, appears old, with every carriage covered in graffiti. Rick, Monica, and I eventually board the train; as we expect, it's standing room only. Huddling close together and keeping our eyes on our bags and our hands on our purses and wallets, we become an attraction for the other passengers. I think we are the only Americans on this train, as I hear Italian spoken, or perhaps it's a Neapolitan dialect. I understand nothing, since my Italian language skills are nil at this time. The rest of the passengers are positioned against one another, packed into the space like sardines. None of them have luggage, so even more reason for us to stand out as tourists. An unpleasant odor engulfs the space around us. I find myself wondering about any Italian laws limiting the number of passengers, but I vaguely recall reading that such laws are nonexistent in Italy.

After the train makes a few stops, we are fortunate enough to find some vacated seats. While we scramble to sit down, we can't all sit together, which is okay. Monica and I are seated not far from the door, and Rick is a few rows away. The utilitarian seats are made of cheap plastic and most of the windows are open, so I assume there is no air conditioning. The train seems more like an old subway car and, from my perspective, looks like it could be one of the originals from the early 1900s. Somewhat nervous and on alert, Monica and I only communicate in whispers to each other. I notice quite a few of the passengers appear to be students, and the rest seem to be working-class people, judging by the way they are dressed. Far from comfortable by any stretch of the imagination, I'm grateful to be traveling with the more experienced sightseers, Rick and Monica.

I can't wait to get to Sorrento, so I can get off this train. Each station we pass is identified by a graffiti-covered sign, and I only recognize the names of a few, such as Ercolano and Torre del Greco. The only redeeming feature of this train trip is the beautiful scenery along the route, such as the wonderful Vesuvius volcano, which looms even closer now.

As soon as the train pulls into the Sorrento station and comes to a stop, its doors open and we disembark with our bulky luggage. We exchange glances and shake our heads.

"Never again. That's one of the worst experiences of my life," Rick says. We all agree that we do not care to repeat the exercise in anxiety and trepidation.

Now it is time to move forward and be positive. We made it here, and we're alive to talk about it. The best part of this saga is that we are now in beautiful Sorrento, the gateway to the Amalfi Coast. The scent of lemons is in the air, and suddenly everything seems to be so much better.

***

The road that winds along the coast from Sorrento to Vietri sul Mare is the Amalfi Coast Road, know to the Italians as Strada Statale 163. Blue SITA buses, bicycles, scooters, and cars own the road here, a motorway that in some places is so narrow that traffic in one direction is forced to stop in order to allow a bus to traverse a steep S-bend and maneuver a sharp corner. I understand that large mirrors are positioned at some of these dangerous bends to facilitate safe passage.

Plenty of passengers develop car sickness and dizziness while traveling on this road. It's the only way to get to Positano and the other towns along the coast, other than by boat. And from my research, I understand the views are nothing short of spectacular. So, I'm eager to experience this trip and hope I can enjoy the ride, despite the motion sickness I was prone to as a child. Monica doesn't feel well today, with symptoms of a cold, and is unable to travel with us, but she encourages Rick and me to go to Positano and Amalfi without her.

We purchase our tickets at the ticket booth near the Circumvesuviana train station and then cross the street to wait for the bus. The price for the one-hour ride to Amalfi is cheap, less than four euros. We plan to get off in Positano and then maybe catch another bus to Amalfi. From my reading, I know that the buses are so crowded during the summer months that travelers often can't board except at the points of origin. But it's October, so perhaps we'll be able to get on and off with ease. "Let's try to sit on the right side," I say to Rick. "I hear that's the side with the best views."

Among the first passengers to board the bus, we're in luck and find vacant seats on the right side—the side that will hug the cliff along the seaside. My point-and-shoot camera is in my hand, and I'm ready for this adventure. "Too bad Monica can't be here with us," I say to Rick.

"I know. I wish she didn't have to miss this. I'm looking forward to it."

The remaining passengers board the bus, and soon we depart for our Amalfi Coast adventure. Too excited to be nervous, I remain fixated on the surrounding scenery as we begin our travel through the city of Sorrento before reaching the coastal road.

The winding Sorrentine peninsula separates the Gulf of Naples on the north from the Gulf of Salerno on the south. The fifty-kilometer Amalfi Coast Road begins on its southern shore. Many Italians vacation on the less-crowded, but equally beautiful, Sorrentine peninsula to escape the tourists during the busy summer months.

The myriad of S-bends and frequent turns reminds me of riding in a van during a trip to Kings Canyon and Sequoia National Parks in California years ago with my husband and two young sons. The sight of the spectacular looming volcano, Vesuvius, confirms my decision to make this journey today, as we swerve around corners and see the jagged, steep cliffs ahead. I am already awestruck, and I'm smiling as I snap away with my camera. I'm grateful that I feel no waves of dizziness which would take away from my exhilaration.

Experiences in Positano

I know the bus trip from Sorrento to Positano takes about an hour, but the time goes by quickly since I am fascinated by the views around every bend. Riding along the cliffs and looking out over the sea is a dream come true, and this experience is everything I've ever envisioned and more.

Our bus rounds one more bend, and Positano comes into view. This vertical city, built into the side of a cliff that hugs the coast, is breathtaking. Now I understand why it's called the Pearl of the Amalfi Coast. It's a postcard-worthy scene, with rows of pastel-colored houses jutting out from the hills and perched precariously all the way down to the beach. The road continues in a serpentine fashion as we move closer to the town. With the bus stopped on top of the hill just above the center of town, the driver announces that we have reached Positano. Following the actions of the majority of the other passengers, Rick and I get off the bus, assuming this is the only stop. Years later I will learn that there is a second stop on the other side of Positano.

Where we are now is known as the Chiesa Nuovo stop, on Via Guglielmo Marconi and opposite Bar Internazionale.

The bus continues along the high road to who knows where, and Rick and I begin our downhill walk into Positano. Positano is a walking town, and only local shuttle buses can navigate the streets here as they are so steep and have endless turns. To really explore Positano, the experience begins at the top where the buses must drop everyone off, and the rest of the way is on foot. I'm in my glory here, taking photos every few hundred feet and shooting every angle possible.

Memories from the 2003 movie *Under the Tuscan Sun* flash into my mind as the road seems familiar, and I try to recognize the balcony that might have been Marcello's apartment and the location of that fateful scene when Diane Lane's character, Frances, learns he has another woman. I later learn that the filming location is one of the balconies of Hotel California, on Via Cristoforo Colombo.

Cars are sandwiched incredibly close to one another along the edge of this narrow two-way street. I wonder how their drivers manage to leave their parking places without hitting the vehicles in front of or behind them. Most of the autos sport numerous dents and dings, and I smile as I realize the way of life here precludes worry about the care and feeding of a car. Pedestrians are walking in the street, even though sidewalks are available, and the pace meets the criterion for slow, as if everyone is enjoying the lifestyle.

I'm absorbing everything I see, and it seems like a fairy tale just to be here in this idyllic place. John Steinbeck described it perfectly in an article published in 1953 by *Harper's Bazaar*:

Positano bites deep. It is a dream place that isn't quite real when you are there and becomes beckoningly real after you have gone. Its houses climb a hill so

11

steep it would be a cliff except that stairs are cut in it. I believe that whereas most house foundations are vertical, in Positano they are horizontal. The small curving bay of unbelievably blue and green water laps gently on a beach of small pebbles. There is only one narrow street and it does not come down to the water. Everything else is stairs, some of them as steep as ladders. You do not walk to visit a friend, you either climb or slide.

As I notice a sign that reads, "Commune di Positano" (City of Positano), and Rick wanders past a row of parked Vespas, I seize on a photo opportunity. "Rick, stand under that sign, please, so I can get a photo. And I see a spot where maybe you can take one of me."

"Okay, Margie, sure," he replies. In fact, multiple photo ops appear as we walk farther down toward the center of town. The road is not a direct route. Instead, it winds around multiple times like a labyrinth between the homes built on innumerable levels. As I traverse the steep, winding streets, I pass by numerous hillside hotels, including Hotel Villa Franca, Hotel Gabrisa, Hotel Conca d'Oro, Casa Le Terrazze, and Palazzo Marzoli Resort. I can't imagine staying at one of them, since getting anywhere would require strenuous uphill and downhill walking on a daily basis. Positano is a shopper's paradise, as there is an abundance of quaint, boutique-type shops. Hand-painted ceramics, clothing, jewelry, and artwork are the main attractions here. The women's clothing stores catch my eye with their white linen offerings hanging outside to lure the interested shopper. Beautiful fashions but way above my budget. Since Positano is a resort, I expect the prices to be higher than in Sorrento, but I'm pleasantly surprised when I stop to admire the art from one of the street vendors closer to the center of town. I find an eight-by-ten watercolor painting of Positano that I love and keep staring at it. Reasonably priced at only twenty euros, I think this painting will make a memorable souvenir, and I am happy with my purchase.

Somewhere along the way, a strange thing happens. I think I hear my name being called. *Who could know my name here, four thousand miles from home?* I ask myself. I don't give it much thought, and Rick and I keep walking. A few seconds later, I hear my name again, the woman's voice louder, from behind me. I turn around this time to look, and I see a woman waving and calling my name. As she moves closer to me, I recognize her as a coworker of mine from Tampa. I can't believe that someone I work with and play cards with on occasion is here in this town of less than four thousand people—on the same day, at the same time, and on the same street.

"Ginny, is that really you? I can't get over this," I say in near disbelief as we approach and hug each other.

"My husband and I are here with some friends on a day trip," Ginny explains. Introductions are made, and after a brief conversation we say goodbye and go our separate ways. I still find the event astonishing. Never in a million years would that happen again.

My brother and I make a turn onto the other main street in Positano, Via Pasitea. This meandering, one-way street eventually becomes Via Cristoforo Colombo on the other side of Positano. As we continue walking down the hill, we arrive in Piazza Mulini and see signs directing us to *la spiaggia* (the beach). My guess is that it's been about forty minutes since we left the bus stop on top of the hill, and now we arrive in

Piazza Flavio Gioia, where the baroque Church of Santa Maria Assunta, with its majolica-tiled dome and famous Byzantine Black Madonna, is located.

"Let's check out this church, Rick," I say, eager to discover what awaits behind the massive front doors. We hurry inside, and despite the less-than-extravagant façade, the interior of this sacred place is impressive with its white marble and gold accents.

The sanctuary and altar areas are adorned with no less than six immense containers filled with white roses, and an exquisite, three-tiered crystal chandelier hangs high above the altar. A priest is standing at the front of the church with a man and woman facing him. It appears as if he is giving them a blessing of some kind. They are dressed in everyday clothes; otherwise, I might wonder if he is marrying them. I understand this is a popular location for destination weddings.

In the back, a grandiose pipe organ stretches all the way to the ceiling. We don't linger here, staying only long enough to say a prayer and observe the beauty of this Positano basilica.

Just down the wide stairs from the church is the famous Ristorante Buca di Bacco. One of the oldest establishments in Positano, this restaurant dates back to the early 1900s. What once began as a simple tavern now attracts celebrities. Rick and I decide to stop for lunch and ask for a table outside on the beach. Once again my mind wanders, and I think of that scene in the movie when Diane Lane has lunch at this same restaurant. Not being foodies, Rick and I choose pasta *pomodoro* (pasta with tomatoes) and *insalata mista* (mixed salad), which turns out to be the perfect choice. The simple food does not disappoint.

While savoring my meal at this idyllic seaside restaurant, I feel the breeze blowing against my face, a sensation I love. The sound of the gentle ocean waves rolling against the shore make this an unforgettable moment for me. Positano's main public beach, like most beaches on the Amalfi Coast, is not sandy but consists of little stones. Nevertheless, it's a beach, and the views from my perspective are stunning. Today is cloudy and the tourist season is nearly over, so the beach is almost devoid of people. Quite a few wooden boats are positioned on the beach, and a fisherman is mending his nets.

Stray cats are part of the landscape in Positano, and a gray-and-white-striped tabby momma cat and her three babies aren't too far away from our table. I assume the prevalence of seafood scraps keeps the cat population well-fed here.

After our relaxing lunch, Rick and I begin the long walk uphill, retracing our steps back to the bus stop. I know I'll be back to this beautiful place again.

I'm enamored with Positano, and although I don't know it now, I will return to this lovely paradise over and over again in the next eleven years. When I'm asked to choose a favorite place in Italy, I find it so difficult, but at some point the Amalfi Coast—and specifically, Positano—becomes my most-desired destination. Given the chance, I always want to return to this magical, serene, heaven on Earth.

***

It's still early—around two o'clock—so we decide to visit Amalfi, which is only a twenty-minute bus ride away. More twisting road embraces the coast, and I get a glimpse of Atrani, another gorgeous seaside town, beneath us. I think I'd like to visit this place sometime, as I understand it is the smallest community in Italy.

Amalfi is the end of the line for the SITA bus, so all of us disembark. If anyone wishes to continue travel along the Amalfi Coast toward Salerno, Amalfi is the origination point for that route. Rick and I roam around on the dock for less than half an hour while we wait for the bus back to Sorrento. Young boys are playing soccer on the beach, and the homes here are, for the most part, painted white rather than in pastel hues. They are built into the hill but are not quite as vertical as they are in Positano. Amalfi, once a powerful maritime republic, piques my interest, and I make a mental note to return when I have more time to explore this town.

***

The year is 2013, and my travels steer me to Positano for the fifth time. Two of these previous trips involve travel with a friend, and one I make as a solo traveler. This time I return again with Rick, and I'm thrilled that Monica joins us for her first visit to Positano.

Since our accommodations this trip are at Hotel Olimpico, not far from Salerno, we avail ourselves of their free shuttle bus to the Port of Salerno at Piazza Concordia. Ferries depart from here several times a day in season, between April and October, for Amalfi and Positano. On the dock, we purchase our round-trip tickets for Positano. The ride is expected to be an hour and fifteen minutes altogether. We realize that we just missed the ferry, so we have to wait an hour for the next one. With plenty of time before our 11:40 a.m. scheduled departure, I keep myself busy taking photos of the coast and marina on this sunny day in southern Italy.

The weather can't be more perfect. Hundreds of sailboats and motorboats are docked here, and it becomes obvious to me that there are also a substantial number of fishing boats, their floors covered in nets. I'm fascinated as I watch a fisherman pull his boat close to the dock to tie it down, and then I observe him as he begins to clean his nets.

Soon it is time for our ferry to leave the port, and I'm treated to a real-life slideshow of the seaside towns at the eastern end of the Amalfi Coast. The first that comes into view is the town of Vietri sul Mare, well-known for its ceramics. Until now, my only view of this place is a glimpse from above while on a SITA bus. The perspective from the sea is completely different, and I'm loving it. So far, Monica shows no signs of seasickness, and both she and Rick are enjoying the view. It takes about thirty-five minutes to reach Amalfi, where the ferry docks to let passengers on and off, and then it's on to Positano. Since that is our destination, we are anxious to arrive, despite the glorious seascapes of the villages of Cetara and Furore in front of us.

Once we get a peek of Positano a few miles out, Monica is taking photos with her iPad, and I'm snapping away with my camera. By one o'clock we arrive in the most famous resort town on the Amalfi Coast. We're content to wander around the beach area and walk up a few of the lower hills where all the boutiques and artsy shops are located. Having no agenda but to enjoy the atmosphere, we stroll at our own pace. A *gelateria* (ice-cream shop) tantalizes us, but we would rather have lunch here. After a while, we find an inviting outdoor restaurant not too far from the beach.

Wine-Dark House is situated in a little piazza near the bottom of the steps which lead up toward the church. The restaurant's name seems unusual to me, but this description on their business card is all the explanation I need: "La casa color del vino" — the wine-colored house. How interesting! The pasta *pomodoro* and green salad are *perfetto* (perfect) for the three of us as we dine outside on this warm, bright afternoon. Just sitting here without being in a rush and taking in everything is the epitome of enjoying *la dolce vita* (the sweet life).

"I can't get that gelato out of mind," I say once our meal is finished. "Do either of you want some?" Rick and Monica decline, but my sweet tooth overrides any concern about healthy eating. *After all, I'm in Italy*, I tell myself, justifying my decision. "Okay, I'll be right back."

I walk around the corner and satisfy my sugar craving by ordering two scoops in a cone, *nocciola* (hazelnut) and *stracciatella* (chocolate-chip) flavors. *Mmmm.* Savoring this cold, sweet treat, I saunter back and finish eating my gelato at the table.

"That looks good," Monica says. Rick acts disinterested, saving his calorie allotment for M&M's later.

"Yes, it's delicious." Calories and carbohydrates are not on my mind at this moment.

After lunch we browse around near the shops some more. We decide to take the 3:30 p.m. ferry back to Salerno, so we still have a little time to wait. We walk over to the beach to watch the people. None of us could have predicted that we would be indulged with some free entertainment, although I'm not so sure I'd pay to see this. A tall, thin, tanned, elderly Italian gentleman appears out of nowhere and parades around the pier area in a light-blue Speedo. I recall seeing him earlier near the shops in town, sporting the same skimpy attire. He doesn't appear to have any purpose other than to be seen. Exhibitionism at its best in Italy. You gotta love the Italians.

Once we arrive back at the port in Salerno, we notice two other Italian men in Speedos near the marina. These men, however, are not thin by any stretch of the imagination, and they are getting onto motorcycles. *Way too much skin for me today.* Monica and I look at each other and just shake our heads. It's a visual I can do without, but now it's etched into my memory forever.

The Island of Capri

The Italian island of Capri is a place known as a resort for the rich and famous. Plenty of movie stars and celebrities vacation here, and aside from its glitz and lavish prices, Capri is an island off the Sorrentine peninsula and close to the Amalfi Coast. A frequent day trip for cruise travelers from Naples, this tiny island, which is only the size of New York's Central Park, is always crowded. Despite the reality, I'm checking it off my bucket list today.

This is the last day in May, 2011, and I'm traveling solo in Italy. The weather is sunny and warm, perfect for a boat trip on the Tyrrhenian Sea. Since I'm staying in Maiori, I take the blue SITA bus to Amalfi, only twenty minutes away. The town of Amalfi is sort of a headquarters for transportation on the Amalfi Coast, and after purchasing a round-trip ferry ticket, I board the double-decker boat along with the rest of the waiting tourists. I position myself on the starboard side of the deck, anticipating spectacular photo opportunities as the ferry passes the towns of Positano, Praiano, and other sights on the ninety-minute trip to Capri.

Once all the passengers board, the ferry leaves the dock and cruises away from land toward our island destination. Thrilled to be on the water once again, I can't control my sense of elation as the wind blows across my face and the warmth of the sun massages my tanned arms. The fresh air of the sea invigorates me, and I want to cherish every moment as I close my eyes and realize how fortunate I am to be here.

I take photos of the sea, the rugged coastline, and even the wake behind the boat, since this is my first experience seeing the Amalfi Coast from this perspective offshore. As we near Positano, the view is like a travel postcard. Thank God for digital cameras, since I am shooting every few seconds as we move closer to the shoreline of the picturesque resort town. Docking near Spiaggia Grande, the ferry allows passengers to disembark before accepting new ones. With such a beautiful scene in front of me, I daydream about staying here forever.

The remainder of the journey doesn't disappoint, as the Amalfi Coast is nothing short of a photographer's delight. Tiny private beaches, secret hidden caves, and terraced groves of lemon trees and grapevines are part of the coastal landscape. I'm awestruck as I see a promontory that miraculously supports a hotel and restaurant, cantilevered over the sparkling deep-blue sea.

Emerging from the sea between Positano and Capri is an archipelago of three islands known as Li Galli. These imposing rocky formations are also known as Le Sirenuse, from *sirena* in Italian. According to Greek mythology, sirens were believed to be half women, half birds. As legend has it, the singing of the sirens distracted the sailors, luring them to their death upon the rocky shore. Indeed, the sea currents in this area are formidable, and boats must cruise the area with great care to avoid crashing.

It's a beautiful sight, regardless of the history. A curious bit of trivia is that Russian ballet dancer Rudolf Nureyev purchased these islands in 1988 and spent his remaining years here.

Soon, Capri appears in my view, and I guess I am naïve, but I'm surprised when it's nothing like I imagine. This huge, rocky island is now directly in front of the boat, and it appears almost mountainous, with steep cliffs, similar to the landscape of the Amalfi Coast. In my mind's eye, up until now, my vision was of a much flatter piece of land. But as I'm learning, little of Italy is flat—and especially in the Campania region.

As my ferry cruises closer to Capri, I am mesmerized by three mammoth rock formations at the southern end of the island. I later learn that these are the Faraglioni Rocks, sometimes known as "sea stacks," and are a result of forceful winds and raging seas. What a grand welcome to Capri!

The waters around this island are a pristine, emerald green, like none I've seen anywhere else. Our ferry captain treats his passengers to a surprise by pulling up close to a few secluded caves where the sunlight is shining in a way that makes the sea sparkle. *Perhaps this is what the Blue Grotto is like*, I think to myself. People from another boat have jumped off and are refreshing themselves in the shallow waters. A guide on the ferry explains that this is Grotto Verde (Green Grotto), and it's named for the reflection of green light on the rocks inside of the cave.

At the end of the journey, the captain docks his ferry in Marina Piccolo, the smaller of the two marinas of Capri. Before we disembark, an enterprising young Italian named

Vincenzo proposes an offer hard to resist. He's charming and attractive, the picture of health with his trim physique. His pitch-black curly hair and dark brown eyes make me think he grew up in the Mediterranean area. In perfect English and with an engaging smile, he convinces me and a few other passengers to let him take us on a walking tour for twenty euros. I usually don't like organized tours, and I also had the idea to see the Blue Grotto on my own. But after Vincenzo explains that I'd have to take two buses there and back, and a lot of time would be spent for an experience that might last two or three minutes, I opt to go with him. With that captivating smile, he promises to show our group all around Capri, as well as the higher town of Anacapri, and non-touristy sights I probably would miss on my own. In addition, he says we will have free time, and he can recommend restaurants and places not to miss. This turns out to be a good decision.

True to reports, Capri is crowded, but I'm enjoying it, and a gelato is refreshing on this hot morning as I wander around during my free time. At a prearranged time and meeting spot, Vincenzo collects our group in a minibus and announces that we are going to experience the "Mamma Mia" road as he drives us up to Anacapri. He lovingly refers to us as his "family" and seems to take immense joy as he prepares us for the nine-minute, white-knuckle experience on the serpentine, two-and-a-half-mile road up the steep hill. The views along the way are spectacular, even more so than from Capri down to the marina. I don't know what to expect in Anacapri, but I'm eager to go on this adventure.

Once in Anacapri, as Vincenzo predicted, the panorama from nine hundred feet above the sea is even more captivating. Much less congested than Capri, Anacapri seems more relaxed, yet equally as charming. Vincenzo suggests lunch at Barbarossa Restaurant, and when he tells us he is eating there too, I assume it must be good. I opt to follow his recommendation, and I am not disappointed, as the food is delicious and the price is reasonable.

I enjoy wandering around the town and browsing the many family-run shops, taking in the ambience and not feeling as if I have an agenda. This day doesn't allow enough time to adequately visit the famed Villa San Michele, so I make a mental note to return. Vincenzo also mentioned the funicular ride to Monte Solaro, and although I pass by its entrance, I decide to forgo that too. *I can always return and spend more time,* I tell myself. I don't realize it at the time, but exactly a year later I find myself back in Anacapri.

***

It's now May, 2012, and I'm on a Mediterranean cruise, traveling with my friend Sue. Our fun memories from our first cruise around Italy two years earlier persuade us to travel together again. Cruise Critic, a cruise review community website, features online message boards that allow cruise passengers to post messages months before the date of departure, so they can engage with other passengers who have booked the same cruise. Since I enjoy travel planning, I decide to organize a personalized, small-group excursion for eight from the port of Naples to several of the Sorrentine villages with Pleasant Travel, a local tour agency.

At seven thirty in the morning, our group of eight meets on the dock, and I see Mariano Fiorentino, the owner and operator of Pleasant Travel, waiting for us. He is holding a sign with my name on it. Instant relief floods through me as I realize that the email arrangements for today's excursion prove to be successful. This smiling, middle-aged, balding man wearing a navy-blue cardigan trimmed in burgundy introduces himself and directs us to his waiting vehicle.

The weather is perfect—a bit cool this morning but the sun is shining, and the sea air is invigorating. Sue and I, along with three married couples we previously met at the Meet and Greet on the ship, climb into Mariano's air-conditioned Mercedes van, and he whisks us away for what will prove to be a fantastic day.

Mariano is a native of this area, born in the nearby village of Piano di Sorrento, and he is the perfect person to take us to visit these little-known places. Fluent in English, he has stories to tell, and I am reminded of his great sense of humor. His personality matches the name of his company, as he is always smiling and laughing. I'm familiar with Mariano since I organized a tour with his company a couple of years ago. He is definitely the one to call for another unforgettable experience.

"I'm going to take you to the smaller towns on the Sorrentine peninsula, and we will have a good time. After that, we'll drive farther down the Amalfi Coast so you can see beautiful Positano from the road, okay?"

This sounds like a wonderful plan to me, and Sue and some of the others agree. "We're ready to go," I say.

Our group interacts well, and everyone is enthused about the plan for the day. I think a small-group excursion like this is so much better than a larger excursion on a tour bus. Mariano lets us know that he is happy to stop along the way, promising lots of opportunities for photos at choice locations. I think he enjoys photography as much as I do, because we aren't even out of Sorrento yet when he pulls the van to the side of the road and lines us up for our first group photo with a view of Vesuvius behind us. I like it already.

About twenty minutes later, we stop at another overlook high above the city for a quick photo with Sorrento in the background. I think he's done this a few times. Mariano seems to relish providing us with numerous chances to capture awesome photos with amazing vistas. He even lines us up at an overlook so we can take another group shot. I think these are his favorite. He offers to shoot the snapshots, orchestrating the position of each person to obtain the best group photograph, and accommodating each of us, using several of our cameras.

Once back in the van, Mariano navigates the winding road like a pro as we make our way to the first of the little towns. Within ten minutes, we reach his hometown, Piano di Sorrento, and he stops the van to chat with a man who is about to make a delivery of fresh mozzarella. I love this, as we experience the local flavor and listen to the language while the two men converse with each other. No hurry here, just as it should be in this beautiful part of Italy. Surrounded by the natural beauty of the Campania region, I could not be any happier. After a ten-minute stop, we're back on the curvy road and pass terraced lemon groves that can be seen all the way down to the sea. Green netting covers the trees, and Mariano points out the land that still belongs to his family.

Then he announces he has a surprise for us. A few minutes later, he parks across the uncrowded street and tells us to wait as he goes into a *negozio di alimentari* (food store).

"I wonder what he's doing?" someone says.

After five minutes, Mariano comes out of the store to tell us we may have to wait about ten more minutes. None of us mind, and by now we already know that nothing happens fast in Italy.

"They're almost finished making the mozzarella, and I want you to taste it fresh," he informs us with a smile and gleam in his eye. *So that's the surprise! How lucky can we be?*

Now everyone is commenting on the good fortune to have a guide like Mariano, who knows all the shop owners in his town and offers us an experience we could never duplicate back in the States. Before long, Mariano returns with a package wrapped in white paper and we are off to the next town, Termini.

He buys this *formaggio* (cheese) for us as a special treat since he wants us to taste it while we are here with him. When we reach the next town, he parks and announces we are taking a break for half an hour to soak in the natural wonders and, of course, to pose for yet another panoramic photo. While we're taking our own photos, Mariano stays behind for a few minutes and then emerges with his hands full as he approaches our group. Like a waiter who is proud to present the chef's signature dish, he serves us the fresh mozzarella on white paper plates and hands each of us a white napkin.

It's my first time tasting mozzarella that is only an hour old. I quickly realize how special and different this is, as it melts in my mouth. We all agree that the just-made, local cheese is some of the best mozzarella any of us has ever eaten. Elated, Mariano watches us devour this special surprise of his.

As the others finish their cheese and enjoy the view, I have time to wander on my own. Three local butchers who are standing outside in front of their shop greet me with smiles as I approach them with a request. "Si," they say, nodding with enthusiasm when I ask permission to take a photo of them in front of their shop. I love meeting the locals in Italy and always find them to be happy people.

Back in the van, we continue our trip as Mariano guides us through a couple of other towns, including Massa Lubrense and Sant'Agata. Once more, he stops the van and takes out an enlarged, colorful map of the area, so we can see exactly where we have gone. *How thoughtful he is.* He continues the drive on the Amalfi Coast until we near Positano, and the views are stunning. Today, though, there isn't time to visit this resort town, so we turn around and make our way back on the same road toward Sorrento. This trip is something I hold dear, and I am thankful for all the photos capturing the sheer beauty of this experience, in case my memory fails me in the future.

After we arrive back in Sorrento, our group separates. Sue and I plan to grab a bite to eat before it's time to leave for Capri, our planned afternoon excursion. Two of our group decide to spend the rest of the afternoon in Sorrento and will take a ferry back to the port of Naples later on their own. Mariano offers to drive the rest of us to the pier, where we plan to catch a hydrofoil to the island of Capri.

"You go ahead and shop for a little while," he says. "I will go to the dock to check the schedules at the marina. Then I'll come back and let you know the details and ticket prices." We arrange a meeting point and time with him and wave goodbye.

When he picks us up at the prearranged time, he shares all the information about the best departure time and where to buy the tickets. He also suggests that it would be best to purchase a round-trip ticket now for the trip back to Naples later in the afternoon. I'm also grateful he recommends the latest ferry time we should book for our return to Naples so we don't miss the ship. *I think this man is a saint.*

***

We have no problems purchasing tickets and securing seats on the hydrofoil to Capri. Once we arrive at Marina Grande, I remember that we need to take a bus to the center of Capri and then another bus or a taxi to Anacapri. I'm determined to ride that chairlift to Monte Solaro in Anacapri today. We start walking into town, and not far from the pier, we are in luck as we meet Alessandro, a good-looking, tanned taxi driver, wearing sunglasses and a smile and sporting a fashionable turquoise sweater over a white-collared shirt. Very easy on the eyes. He offers to drive the six of us to the center of Capri for twenty euros—a bargain when split six ways. Within seconds we're climbing into his very cool white Nissan Serena Capri open taxi. I've never seen such a chic taxi, but this is the land of luxury where they cater to the lifestyles of the rich and famous.

Once we are all inside the taxi, Alessandro proposes a second offer, this one to take us on a tour of Anacapri as well, including free time in both locations, for twenty euros per person. I realize his offer is well worth the cost, having taken a similar tour with Vincenzo a year ago, but I don't want to repeat my experience. "I think I'll just go on my own and will meet up with the rest of you later," I say as I encourage them to accept the offer.

My companions, however have other ideas. A bond has formed between all of us, and after some back-and-forth conversation, they convince me to go along. My change of heart is based on two things: I believe it is more fun to explore with people I enjoy. And the second reason, maybe more important than the first, is Alessandro himself. He is quite charming, and I appreciate his subtle, no-pressure sales pitch. He lives in Capri, and it certainly doesn't hurt that he looks like he belongs on the cover of *GQ* magazine. *What better taxi driver could we have?*

Within minutes, Alessandro adeptly drives us up the Mamma Mia road to Anacapri, the town high above Capri. Choruses of "Ciao, Alessandro" ring out as we wave goodbye, having arranged a meeting time for our return trip to the marina later. Next, all six of us head straight to the Monte Solaro chairlift. For the totally-worth-it price of ten euros, I am going to experience what will turn out to be the highlight of my trip to Italy!

Sue commits to riding the chairlift, despite some apprehension.

"I've never gone skiing before or been on a chairlift, and I'm a little scared too," I say, doing my best to reassure her. "But it's not enough to keep me from doing it. The views will be so worth it." This time I'm resolute, no matter how scared I might be. I'm not going to miss my opportunity to see Capri and the Bay of Naples from 2000 feet above sea level. I'm putting fear aside and going for it.

We encourage each other, and we're ready for this challenge. Observing that the chairs are only large enough to seat one person at a time, I also notice that they do not stop, so I have to be ready to hop on as soon as it's my turn. My heart is beating fast, and I'm keyed up.

Success! I'm on. The single steel bar that comes across doesn't lock, so for a split second, I panic. But I tell myself that hundreds, if not thousands, of people ride this every day, so it must be safe. As the chair begins its climb, I look out over the sea and breathe in the fresh, cool air. A sense of calm begins to envelop me. The slow, twelve- or thirteen-minute ascent becomes awe-inspiring, serene, and quiet. Any fears dissipate, and I'm able to fully appreciate the solitude and tranquil environment as I absorb the spectacular view beneath me. Even though I'm climbing higher into the air, the chairlift is never that far off the ground. I'm gazing at everything, overjoyed to stare at the sea and look at the houses of the town from this aerial perspective. The higher I go, the smaller everything appears. In the distance, the boats anchored offshore look like tiny white eggs. The stillness at this height imparts an almost surreal sense, as if nothing matters but this moment. *Il dolce far niente* (the sweetness of doing nothing)! My mind is clear and I'm fully present. I don't hear the waves below, but I hear chirping of birds in a muted way.

The only other time in my life when I've experienced anything similar is one occasion years ago, when I floated on air high above Port Lucaya in the Bahamas on my solo parasailing endeavor. I remember the initial exhilarating rush as I lifted off the platform and the absolute quiet and sense of peacefulness as I hovered four hundred feet above the ocean, all by myself, for seven minutes — an unforgettable sensation that equals this instant, a priceless once-in-a-lifetime memory. This is paradise, and as much as I look forward to reaching Monte Solaro, I'd will this moment to last forever if I could.

But nothing lasts forever, and the end of the ride is in sight, so I prepare myself to be ready to jump off. I arrive at Monte Solaro and feel solid ground beneath my feet. As I look past the chairlift area, I realize that I have reached the highest point on the island of Capri, 1,932 feet above sea level. I momentarily forget about everything else.

The panoramic views from the top are magnificent, encompassing both the gulfs of Napoli and Salerno. Spellbound, I wander to all points accessible in this limited mountaintop area and linger as long as possible so I can immerse myself in this place, to fully soak in the scene. My camera is in hand, of course.

Close by, La Canzone Del Cielo serves wine, gelato, and snacks on a shaded outside terrace. Delighted to be welcomed this way, I'm eager to relax here for a while with my travel companions. The sun is intense, so this little bar is the perfect place to enjoy a gelato, and I choose pistachio and *stracciatella* in a cup. I also find clean restrooms here.

I'm told that this oasis at one time had a swimming pool, and a large solarium still exists. Having originally been built in the 1950s, I can't imagine how much effort it would be to haul construction equipment up here.

After a while, it's time to leave, and we all head over to the chairlift. No trepidation this time. The descent down is as beautiful as the ride up, and I notice the gardens in people's yards, with flowers blooming and vegetables almost ready for harvest. For me, this is the best day since arriving in Italy this trip.

Afterward I have time to browse the shops in Anacapri before Alessandro picks us up. At the prearranged time, we meet him and his taxi, and he drives us to the lower town of Capri, where he leaves our group to shop to our hearts' content and spend some more free time on our own. I am impressed by the luxurious Grand Hotel Quisisana, with its stunning grand entrance and various countries' flags displayed from an expansive balcony. Celebrities are known to stay here, and I can imagine how exorbitant the cost of a three-night stay might be.

Just before it's time to leave to meet Alessandro at the pickup point, I am almost blown away by what's in front of me. I can hardly believe what I see as I stare ahead. On a stone wall at the entrance to town is a huge poster-like sign advertising a restaurant in big blue letters. The name of the restaurant is Longano, my maiden name. The wording on the poster is: "Ristorante – Pizzeria LONGANO *Forno a legna di quercia*" (oak wood oven). The address is Via Longano, 9 Piazzetta di Capri. And the hook is, "low prices, 50 types of pizza." I'm intrigued and, at the same time, a bit frustrated, since not enough time is left for me to retrace my steps to find Longano Restaurant. *If only I had another hour.* I guess I will be forced to return to Capri yet another time.

The reliable and punctual Alessandro arrives in his taxi and takes us to our final destination close to the port, where he drops us off in time to board the 4:30 p.m. hydrofoil to Naples. The ferry is packed, and while we all manage to find seats, sitting together is out of the question. Quite a luxurious boat, the hydrofoil's interior resembles the inside of an airplane, with carpeting and seating of similar design. Compared to the utilitarian car ferries I've experienced on Lake Como, this one surpasses those a hundredfold. I keep reminding myself that I am, after all, in Capri, where the real estate is said to be the most expensive in the world. Seated inside this huge boat, I close my eyes and visualize everywhere I've been in the past few hours. *Bliss.*

Ceramics of the Amalfi Coast

Of all the made-in-Italy products I love, the handcrafted ceramics are definitely a favorite. Specific regions in Italy are famous for production of these colorful items, and the places that first come to mind for me are Deruta, Orvieto, Caltagirone, and Vietri sul Mare. Deruta and Orvieto are in Umbria; Caltagirone is in Sicily; and Vietri sul Mare is on the Amalfi Coast. The ceramics created in each place are usually identifiable by color choices and designs. While other places in Italy produce the handcrafted majolica ceramics, Vietri sul Mare is known throughout the world as a top producer of ceramics. But it is the one place I have yet to go.

A full-size baker's rack in my kitchen at home is filled with Italian ceramics, keepsakes from my travels to these towns, and I don't have much room for more purchases. I do have one diminutive purple-and-yellow plate from Vietri, a thoughtful gift and souvenir from the manager of Hotel Olimpico.

During a 2015 trip to Positano and an elaborate lunch at the Michelin-starred La Sponda restaurant at Le Sirenuse Hotel, I smile when I recognize the familiar Vietri designs of fish, turtles, ducks, and other animals on the plates painted in the colors of the Mediterranean. The designs are fun and a conversation starter, for sure. Each plate is edged in white with different-colored dots. I also recall seeing this design on an episode of The Food Network's *Giada in Italy*, when Giada De Laurentiis cooked in Positano. This popular design from Vietri is known as *campagna*, and I remember thinking how much I'd love to have a set of dinnerware like these.

During that same trip I buy two little plates at a shop in Positano. The prices are fairly reasonable, but that is all I can safely carry home, due to the weight restrictions of carry-on bags within Italy. I'd never trust handmade ceramics in my checked bags, for fear they'd break.

Once I'm home my wish list doesn't fade, and I begin searching on the internet for these plates. To my surprise, I find them on Facebook from someone named Romeo Cuomo, and his post includes a photo of various sizes of plates with exactly the same designs as the ones I have from Positano. No surprise, because mine were made in Vietri. The writing on the back of the plates says, "Cassetta Vietri per alimenti Positano." Translated to English, this means the plates are made by an artisan named Cassetta from Vietri, and the plates are for food, and made for a shop in Positano. It seems natural for restaurants and shops on the Amalfi Coast to feature ceramics made in nearby Vietri.

After a few emails back and forth with Romeo, whose business is in Vietri, he quotes me a price for twenty plates in my choice of color and design. The shipping charge is reasonable for the weight, and within a month, a huge box arrives at my home, just in time for Christmas. *Santa is good to me indeed.* Impeccably wrapped, the shipment arrives intact with no breakage. To thank me for the business, Romeo extends a generous offer to me of a personalized, guided tour of the artisans' workshops whenever I come to Vietri. So I decide to make that part of my agenda when I return to my beloved Amalfi Coast the following year.

***

Now it's October of 2016, and I'm setting aside part of a day to go to Vietri and meet Romeo. My communication is mostly with his American business partner, Terri Affanato, who splits her time between Italy and the States. We agree on the date and time, and since I'm staying in Positano once again, I wake up early and have just enough time for breakfast before I have to walk up the hills to the Sponda bus stop. Few people are wandering around this early, and I assume they are the locals on their way to work. I pass a person I recognize as a waiter from my hotel, and he nods. Most of the tourists are probably asleep, and I embrace this change of scenery in the quiet morning hour. I know my way around this town quite well by now, and the twenty-five-minute hike is nothing like the very first time I tried to navigate these steep, inclined walkways. I arrive at the bus stop twenty minutes early and find a stray dog asleep on the bench, to the disgust of a local woman. In Italian she complains to me that he is always sleeping on this spot. "Questo cane dorme sempre qui ogni giorno." I find the situation amusing, but then I'm a tourist and don't live here. I smile and shake my head in response. The bus is a few minutes late, arriving at nine thirty, and I'm grateful to have a seat. Once more, I sit on the right side for the view and am almost blinded by the brilliance of the sun's reflection off the sea at this early morning hour. *Let the day begin.*

This bus stops in Amalfi but just late enough for me to miss the 10:00 a.m. bus to Vietri, so I have time to kill before the 11:00 a.m. bus. Eager for more exercise and photo possibilities, I wander around Amalfi for a while and then return to the bus area so I can be one of the first to board. Since this is the origination point, I anticipate it may be crowded, and I don't relish the thought of standing for an hour.

I have instructions from Terri to meet in the center of Vietri near the bus stop at noon, and I am hoping I can find the location without too much trouble. We are communicating via Facebook Messenger, so I'm glad I have a data plan for my smartphone for the times Wi-Fi isn't available. I'm loving the ride, but I'm more enthusiastic about getting to Vietri to see the authentic Italian ceramic artisans at work. The chance to go behind the scenes and learn about the ceramics process firsthand is a thrill for me.

Exactly at noon, I arrive in Vietri at a busy part of town, where buses, cars, and Vespas converge from several streets and pedestrians seem to be everywhere. As soon as I step off the bus, my fears dissipate as I see a woman dressed in a pretty floral blouse, smiling and waving to me. I knew this must be Terri, and within seconds we introduce ourselves with the typical *due baci e un abbraccio* (two kisses and a hug). Romeo is nearby, as well as Terri's sister, Dee, and brother-in-law, Jon, who are visiting from Massachusetts. Everyone seems very friendly, and I take an instant liking to them, as they do their best to help me feel as if I am part of the family.

Romeo is exactly how I envisioned him. He is passionate about what he does and seems to know everyone here. Dressed in a gray fleece long-sleeved shirt and blue jeans, he seems like an everyday kind of guy.

"Piacere di conoscerla, Romeo," I say, trying my best to use the Italian I know as I tell him how happy I am to meet him in person. Romeo speaks some English, but Terri translates for him.

The five of us begin a short walking tour along the streets of Vietri as we head toward the ceramic artisans' shops. I am overwhelmed by the abundance of ceramic tiles, pots, doorframes, signs, and shops everywhere I turn. I'm reminded of my visits to Caltagirone, the Sicilian city of ceramics, which must have over a hundred ceramic shops, and most everything in the historic center is made of ceramics.

Here in Vietri everything seems more compact, and since it's Saturday, the town is full of people. I don't think I can walk five feet without hues of blue, yellow, red, and green showering my senses. Each shop's name is created on ceramic tiles, and the entire façade of that shop is decorated in multicolored designs of the artist's choice. Large decorative pots adorn the entrances, and lovely flowering plants in vases on the sidewalks entice shoppers. Brilliant colors blast past me like a kaleidoscope as I follow Romeo and Terri down the tapered streets. Jon and Dee follow at their own pace. "It's Saturday, so the shops are closed," Romeo explains, "but I've asked a few artisans to open just for you."

I'm touched and almost moved to tears, thinking that each of these Vietri artists are giving up their day off for me to see them work. Nothing can compare to a personal experience where you meet the locals. "Grazie mille, Romeo. Lo apprezzo." (Thank you very much, Romeo. I appreciate that.) He nods and then stops to talk with local residents and artists, mingling with those who work for him with obvious camaraderie. Soon we arrive at our first stop, the workshop of one of the female ceramics artists. The sign outside her workshop reads, "Romolo Apicella Ceramica a Vietri di Anna Rita Cassetta."

"We're going to meet the artist who made your dishes," Terri announces with a gleam in her blue eyes as she smiles at me. I think Terri is as eager to see my reaction as I am.

"Wow, I had no idea. This is more than I could have expected. I'm so excited."

The writing on the back of my ceramic plates is the same as the sign. I can hardly wait to meet my artist!

I peek inside the tiny shop, and Anna Rita is sitting against a wall in a tiny corner, her head down, eyes intent on her work. Her short, wavy, coal-black hair is accented by her hoop earrings and the chic Italian eyeglasses perched on the end of her nose. In a stylish black sweater, she is the epitome of an artist.

Surrounded by many pots of paint and numerous paintbrushes in a tight space, Anna Rita focuses with precision as she details a ceramic piece with a thin brush in her right hand, stabilizing a turntable with her left. After a few seconds, she pauses to look up at me, and introduces herself with a smile.

"I'm so pleased to meet you, Anna Rita," I say. "Mi chiama Margie." She engages in some conversation in Italian with Terri and Romeo for a few minutes, and then we leave her to her work. She agrees to pose for a photo at my request before we bid her arrivederci. Such a sweet lady.

Although my hope is to purchase some ceramics today, Terri explains that the process doesn't work that way here. "These artisans create everything as custom orders. All the pieces on display in their showroom, or in here, are already spoken for. If you want to order any, I can ship the ceramics to you. Romeo is going to take us to the showroom later, but first we're going to meet another artist."

Romolo Apicella Ceramics is an Italian pottery workshop, with a historical tradition of over half a century. The other artisan I am about to meet also works for the Romolo Apicella group.

A few streets away and around a couple of corners, we arrive at another little workshop, where I have the pleasure of meeting Raffaele, an older, gray-haired gentleman, whose prominent cheekbones and Italian nose make me think he's broken a few ladies' hearts in his lifetime. He takes pride in telling us in Italian that he is seventy years old and has been creating Vietri pottery since the age of nine. Dressed in stripes of blue and gray, with a collared shirt and an inside-out apron, Raffaele's sleeves are rolled up to his elbows, his hands covered in potter's clay. As I glance around his workspace, I notice piles of gray clay in various shapes, some still packaged in clear plastic. Surrounding Raffaele are shelves filled with pottery that is not yet painted.

On the table in front of him are a few pieces of the clay which, I learn, originates in the quarries in the province of Salerno. Raffaele is eager to demonstrate his skills for us. I'm thrilled to be able to experience him creating something artistic right in front of my eyes. I ask permission to take a video, and Raffaele smiles and nods. Then he begins working with the clay. He turns on the power to his electric turntable and, within seconds, uses his hands to form a perfectly shaped bowl. With skill achieved only from a lifetime of experience, he uses both hands to shape this bowl into a taller object, which I first think might become a vase. Every ten seconds or so, he adds small amounts of water and works with meticulous care to complete his design. In less than a minute, he finishes and picks up the flawlessly formed pitcher, holding it up for our approval. I am blown away and would love to stay here all day and watch this artist at work.

Later I learn that Raffaele is loved dearly by the local people of Vietri. Alfonso Vincenzo Mauro, consultant/advisor at Vietri's Department of Tourism and Culture and a native of Vietri, shares his thoughts with me: "What a man! In Vietri we love him and affectionately nicknamed him Filuccio (li'l Raffaele), now one of the oldest ceramics masters still alive."

Before Terri and Romeo usher us out, I notice the variety of the clay objects inside the workshop. One large piece grabs my attention, and I realize that artisans like Raffaele are not simple craftsmen, but true artists. The piece is a statue that stands about three feet high. Its base is a giant fish adorned with a sea star and another fish attached to its body. A beautiful mermaid playing a lyre sits atop the fish. It's no wonder this quotation from Saint Francis is on the website of Romolo Apicella:

The one who works with his hands is a worker.
He who works with his hands and his head is a craftsman.
The one who works with his hands, his head and his heart is an artist.
– Saint Francis

We make a quick stop to see the showroom of Anna Rita's ceramics, and Romeo introduces us to Alfredo, a smiling young Italian who manages this aspect of the business. Here, I can see the brightly colored finished ceramic pieces, although as Terri explained earlier, they are for display and can only be ordered for delivery later. *I'll take one of each, please.*

By now, Terri and Romeo decide it's time for some lunch, and they know the best places — where the locals go, of course. Wine, appetizing food, conversation, and laughter dominate our midday break at an appealing outdoor restaurant, and then it's back to serious business as we head to the factory where the ceramics are made. A bit away from the historic center of town, the ceramics factory is a short drive from here. The factory is also closed today, but thanks to Romeo's connections with the owner, we are able to go inside this industrial-looking building. A nearby sign reads, "Ceramica Artistica Artigianale," and colorful artists' renderings, like a storyboard on ceramic tiles, depict various stages of work in the pottery business.

Romeo enters the structure while our group waits outside a few minutes. Soon he ushers us inside, where I find myself in an impressive ceramics studio that encompasses more than one room. It is filled with elaborate finished pieces of ceramic murals, tabletops, and true works of art, even sculptures. Ceramic tiles in various shapes and designs are in little piles, and walls are covered in tiled designs created by these Vietri artisans. While I'm admiring the art, mesmerized by the immensity and complexity of what surrounds me, a voice interrupts my dreamlike trance.

"This is Antonio," Romeo says as he introduces us to a pleasant young man with medium-length black hair, twinkling brown eyes, and a great smile. With arms around each other, these men share a camaraderie that goes back quite a few years. Antonio shows us some of the more elaborate projects with much pride. Again, these ceramics pieces are custom orders from purchasers, many of whom are commercial buyers. Antonio explains that this is the oldest factory of hand-produced and hand-decorated ceramics still in production in Vietri. His factory has been in continuous operation since the sixteenth century. Together with his father, Antonio Siani owns and operates this company named CE.AR. Antonio and seven others are the only employees.

Terri guides us down a set of steep stairs, warning us to walk with caution as we descend into the working factory. Gone are the brightly colored, shiny ceramics, and in their place are kilns, workshop-style fluorescent lights, and racks of unprocessed tiles.

An occasional religious ceramic statue occupies a shelf in an unobtrusive manner, and colorful crucifixes adorn the walls inside the factory as well as outside. Antonio explains that molded objects first must dry so all the residual water in the clay can evaporate. This is accomplished by exposure to air.

A mammoth drying rack that appears to have been made by hand sits on wheels and, at the right time, is pushed into a giant kiln, where the tiles bake at temperatures of 1000 degrees Celsius for approximately twelve hours. After an additional twenty-four hours, the baked tiles are cool enough for glazing, which is done by immersing the tiles into a solution of enamel to coat the surface. After that, the decoration is applied by hand by skilled ceramic masters. When this artistic process is complete, the tiles or objects are placed back in the oven for a second firing for an additional eight to ten hours at 920-950 degrees Celsius. Another eight to ten hours of cooling is required before the process is complete. Nothing is mass produced here, and just like when it began in the fifteenth century, everything is still made upon request, so each item is unique. I now have a better understanding why these ceramic plates and other items can be as costly as they are. Somehow, though, Romeo and Terri are able to keep prices reasonable.

Antonio seems to enjoy talking with all of us and never gives the impression that he is in a hurry. What is most apparent is that this talent of his is part of his DNA, and he beams with pride, even when he volunteers to share with us some unfinished pieces with which he isn't one hundred percent satisfied. The encounter is personal and can't be replicated anywhere else, on any other day. Thank you so much, Terri and Romeo, for this once-in-a-lifetime experience.

I have purchased ceramics from both of them online and could not be happier with the experience. I'm very satisfied with the shipping and handling of both purchases and highly recommend these two, based on my personal experiences and communication. Every time I use my dishes from Vietri I have an instant memory of my day in Vietri sul Mare.

Meeting People – Memorable Experiences

Every time I hear church bells ringing, see flower boxes on windowsills of ancient buildings, smell the aroma of fresh lemons around me, feel the soft leather of sandals made by hand, or taste fresh homemade pasta, I know why I love Italy.

Besides these reasons — and the architecture, the history, the culture, the beauty, the fashion, the food, and the diversity of the landscape, from the sea to the mountains — I appreciate a conversation with a local Italian. When someone takes time to share their perception of life in Italy with me, I gain knowledge and a better understanding of how it is to actually live in Italy.

What I value more than anything is interacting with the Italian people. My love for Italy stems from a certain sense I first noticed during my visit in 2007. I remember feeling like I was at home. It is the friendliness of the Italian people that motivates me to return again and again, be it for a month or only a few nights. For those who have never been to Italy, this notion may be difficult to understand.

My ongoing love affair with the Amalfi Coast is comprised of numerous encounters and situations. Chance meetings with some special people remain close to my heart and are engraved in my memory forever. I'd like to introduce you to a few of them through my stories.

High above Positano, not far from the hamlet of Monterpertuso, is Nocelle, a *frazione* (hamlet) of Positano. Nocelle is at the end of the Sentiero degli Dei, the hiking trail known as the Path of the Gods, which begins in Agerola and traverses the Lattari Mountains. Until recently, the only way to reach Nocelle was by this pathway, still used by mules, or a set of fifteen hundred steps. Today, bus service exists between these hilltop locations with breathtaking views high above the Tyrrhenian Sea and Positano.

Amalia Durazzo is an Italian woman who lives in Nocelle, and she is the owner of Villa Antica Macina, a beautiful B&B with a terrace that overlooks the Amalfi Coast. Through the white, wrought iron, open gate of her place, I notice two containers filled with beautiful, ripe tomatoes on the steps of what appears to be a house. I see a photo opportunity without realizing where I am, and as I'm composing the picture, I hear a voice say, "Go ahead. Take the picture."

I turn toward the voice to see a woman smiling at me. She has short, curly, brown hair and is dressed in a black-and-white button-down sweater and black pants. She sports a white shoulder-strap purse across her chest and carries a white plastic grocery bag.

"Buongiorno, signora. Mi chiama Margie," I say, introducing myself. Then in English, I continue. "I saw these tomatoes and thought it would make a nice photo. Is this your house?"

The woman introduces herself as Amalia, and she encourages me to take all the photos I like. Her English is excellent, and with a native Italian accent, her voice is pleasing. "I was just going out, but please come in. Go and see the garden." With an enthusiasm and kindness that I've come to know as a trait of Italians, Amalia turns back toward her casa, eager to show me the garden and yard with its colorful flowers, inviting chaise lounges, and an ancient olive press that dates back to the thirteenth century. Indeed, the scene is welcoming.

"Come and see the terrace. What beautiful views we have," she says as she escorts me, her expansive smile revealing her sense of pride. The wide terrace, decorated with white chairs and an umbrella table, is lovingly landscaped, with well-tended, colorful flowers in terra-cotta pots. A separate sitting area is furnished with white outdoor chairs and a divan adorned with purple cushions.

"Oh my God, grazie, this is amazing. The view from here is spectacular," I say. She points out Capri and the Li Galli islands. The panoramic view almost takes my breath away. I explain to her that this is my first time in Nocelle, and that I came upon her place after hiking the Path of the Gods. The atmosphere on her terrace is so serene, truly a place I could enjoy for days and find inspiration to write. We spend some time chatting, and she allows me to photograph her but insists on taking my photo too. I'm sweaty from my four-hour hike and am aware my hair must look a mess—probably frizzy, even in a ponytail—but I acquiesce.

"Where do you stay?" she asks me.

"I'm staying in Positano, on the beach. I came here to write."

"Ah, this is a perfect place to write," Amalia replies. Then she mentions that this is her B&B, once a traditional country home that has been recently renovated, and that there are three rooms. "Come in. I want to show you."

The overwhelming generosity of the Italian people never ceases to surprise me. This is not the first time a complete stranger has offered to share their home, a meal, or a story with me during my travels in Italy. Curious to see the interior of this B&B, I follow Amalia inside. My first impression is how immaculate everything is, and the décor is inviting, with bright colors that blend well with each other. There are three apartments, aptly decorated and named: the Blue Room, the Green Room, and the Yellow Room. Each apartment can accommodate up to four people. Modern amenities and up-to-date furnishings make this an ideal accommodation for anyone who wants to enjoy the pristine atmosphere of the Amalfi Coast, without the hustle and bustle of the more crowded center of Positano.

I thank Amalia for her hospitality and let her know I'm headed to Ristorante Santa Croce, a place I understand is known for wonderful food and great views. We walk together along Via Pizzillo, and soon I see a burly young man walking toward us. He is wearing a light blue T-shirt, olive-green cargo shorts, and work boots. His tanned face is accentuated by his hazel eyes, short, curly, brown hair, and a beard. He is leading a mule that is harnessed — a sure sign that it is a work animal and not a pet. Of course, Amalia know everyone in this hamlet of one hundred forty-one people, and we stop to say hello. She introduces me to Icilio, who greets me with a pleasant smile. I ask the name of his mule, and, with Amalia translating, I am told the mule is called Cardillo. Icilio's affection for his beloved mule is apparent by the way he pets the animal and holds its head close to him when he agrees to pose for a photo.

Amalia explains the need for pack mules on these narrow walkways that are not much wider than sidewalks and often include steep stairways. She informs me that Icilio operates a business with twenty mules which are used in the transportation of luggage, materials, food, and farmers' produce along these rocky paths in the hills. My mind wanders to the idea of construction equipment arriving here to refurbish Amalia's B&B, and I imagine how challenging that would be.

Amalia is such a kind soul. Her smile and her eyes are an open window into her heart. She doesn't know me, yet she invites me to join her for lunch with her husband at their home. In a way, I would love to accept the invitation, but I courteously decline and continue with my plan to eat at Ristorante Santa Croce. I'd like to return one day to this surreal place with the magnificent views and the wonderful woman I'll never forget. I love the people I meet in southern Italy. They all seem so happy despite the hard work their lives entail in a terrain like the hills of the Amalfi Coast.

Before I leave, Amalia tells me she is on Facebook, and we agree to stay in touch. To my surprise, I receive a direct message from her on Facebook the next day, hoping to meet for coffee in Positano before I leave. I'd like that, and I message back, but her schedule gets busy with her guests, and time never allows us to meet again. Maybe the next time I'm in Positano.

***

"Music produces a kind of pleasure which human nature cannot do without." — Confucius

It's my belief that music is a powerful force that can affect one's mood in an instant. For me, music is evocative and makes me feel good. I like almost all kinds of music, from classical, to rock, to opera, to hip-hop. Heavy metal I can do without. But I always enjoy live entertainment. Based on the strong recommendation of another Italophile, I decide to trek up the hill in Positano to a restaurant that features live entertainment on Monday, Wednesday, and Friday nights.

Ristorante Mediterraneo is a family-run dining establishment known for a menu based on fresh, seasonal products and recipes handed down through generations. The atmosphere is informal, and they feature seating indoors as well as outside on a covered terrace. On any given day — unless the weather is bad, of course — I prefer to sit outside, so I request the terrace. I already love the ambience as a friendly young waiter shows me to my table. Whimsical paintings of mermaids adorn the walls, and tables covered in Wedgewood-blue cloths create a comfortable space to enjoy an evening.

Pietro Rainone is due to arrive soon, and I understand he performs for three hours, beginning at seven o'clock. From what I've learned, this native Italian, born in Naples, is an accomplished singer-songwriter, guitarist, and entertainer who has made a career in music for over forty years. His main passion is classic Neapolitan music, and he sings in Italian and English. I'm looking forward to the evening, and so I am in no rush tonight. Before I have a chance to order, a waiter brings me a chilled glass of prosecco and tells me it's complimentary. *How did he know that is exactly what I was getting ready to order?* This place is already exceeding my expectations.

Since I'm dining in a seaside town, I opt for seafood this evening, and choose *gamberoni alla griglia* (grilled prawns). When my meal arrives, I am shocked at the size of the shrimp, as each one must be six inches long. Together with a side dish of *verdure alla griglia* (grilled vegetables), I'm more than satisfied.

As soon as Pietro makes his appearance, the surroundings take on a livelier tone, and the noise level rises to the next decibel. The atmosphere seems charged with electricity, and what's apparent to me is that he truly is a celebrity. With a wide smile that can melt ice and a twinkle in his eye, this sturdy, gray-haired man of about fifty takes instant command of the room. Wearing an untucked, open-collared, striped black shirt, black dress pants, and black Italian leather shoes, he could pass as one of the locals. What sets him apart in appearance, though, is a piece of jewelry around his neck—a chain with a tiny, silver guitar charm. Strapped across his left shoulder is his one-of-a-kind acoustic guitar, decorated with turquoise mermaids playing musical instruments, hand-painted by the same artist who painted the mermaids on the restaurant's walls. Pietro is the epitome of cool.

The attraction of Mediterraneo is its family atmosphere. The waiters and Lorenzo, the manager, seem to get along well and share a camaraderie as they joke around with each other. They even sing along with Pietro, and it's a fun time for everyone. I notice they all are smiling and seem to genuinely enjoy their work. Rodrigo, the tall, thin, attractive host, stands outside much of the time and talks to everyone as they pass by, either in slow-moving cars or on foot. He seems to know everyone, and his gregarious nature makes him a perfect fit for the role. Since Mediterraneo is located on Viale Pasitea, one of the main streets in Positano, traffic can get quite busy, especially on a Friday night like tonight.

Pietro's music is recognizable, as he begins to belt out favorite tunes like "O Solo Mio," "That's Amore," and "Volare." He walks around and plays to the patrons, whom he encourages to sing along. At one point he distributes tambourines, and the show becomes even more of an interactive event. Some of his music is original while other songs are classic favorites, like "Santa Lucia," "Nessun Dorma," and "Quando, Quando, Quando." Switching things up at times, Pietro plays his mandolin for some of the songs, more evidence of his talent and passion for his music.

He also takes time to stop by each table and chat one-on-one, and when he reaches my table, we have a conversation. "Buona sera, Pietro. I am Margie, Margherita. My friend Nancy from Scottsdale told me about you. That's why I'm here, to hear you sing. I'm really enjoying it."

Fluent in his native Italian and English, Pietro replies, "Ciao, Margie. Oh, you know Nancy from Arizona? Yes, we've met before. I play there in the wintertime. You're staying in Positano?"

He is charming and seems genuinely interested to learn more about me. I share with him that I'm a writer and that I'm staying in Positano for two weeks to finish my novel. He tells me a little about his father, who was a famous musician as well. "Do you have a request, a favorite song?"

"Yes, I do. 'Con Te Partirò.' It's my favorite."

"I'll sing it for you a little later. Ciao." And he moves on to the next table. True to his word, a few songs later, he starts to sing the famous Italian song written by Francesco Sartori (music) and Lucio Quarantotto (lyrics). The English translation is "With you I will leave," but it is best known in

English as "Time to Say Goodbye." First performed at the1995 San Remo Festival by Andrea Bocelli, "Con te Partirò" was recorded on his album, *Bocelli*, that same year. The lyrics have such a deep meaning related to loss of a love. The song is also about hope, in that even when you part ways with someone, whether through death or some other reason, the person will remain with you in your heart forever. The powerful song always brings tears to my eyes, as it does now. Pietro makes eye contact with me and makes his way to my table, as if he is singing just to me.

"Grazie, Pietro," I say once he finishes, and I blow him a kiss. I can understand why people fall in love with musicians.

Before the evening ends, I purchase Pietro Rainone's CD, *Bella Italia*, for ten euros—such a bargain. He signs it for me: "2016 A Margherita Baci da Positano Pietro Rainone." The English translation is "2016 To Margherita Kisses from Positano Pietro Rainone." It's a cherished souvenir from Positano that I will treasure forever.

Before my two-week writing trip ends, I need one more music-and-entertainment fix, so I decide to return for another evening of harmonious fun with Pietro Rainone and the Mediterraneo crowd on the following Friday. Walking the more than three hundred steps up the hill is child's play for me now, after being in Positano for almost two weeks. Thank God I am more limber this trip than in previous times. My memories from earlier trips when I had to stop every so often to catch my breath are not pleasant ones. Tonight I arrive a little later, and Pietro is already performing, strolling between the tables, strumming his guitar, and serenading the diners with his classic love songs.

He nods and smiles at me as I enter the restaurant, and I smile back, happy to be recognized and welcomed. I feel like I belong here, and I love the sense of family. I'm seated at an outside table again, under cover since this is the middle of October.

A warm sirocco makes for a comfortable evening. I order a glass of prosecco and an appetizer of bruschetta and settle in for a couple of hours of pure enjoyment. If someone had told me a month ago that I'd be singing along to Italian songs in a restaurant in Positano, I'm not sure I would have believed it. But tonight I am having the time of my life here. I don't mind being alone, because this experience is like being with a big Italian family. But I must admit, when I see couples dining together I can't help but think about how romantic the experience would be if I were sharing this evening with someone I love.

It's a fun place with fun people, and I can see why patrons keep coming back again and again. Before it's time to leave, Pietro poses with me for a photo, and I guarantee he'll see me again when I return on my next visit here. I have no doubt about making that promise come true. Grazie di tutto, Pietro.

Ravello

I hope today isn't the day my childhood tendency toward carsickness reappears, because the road to Ravello has all the switchbacks the Amalfi Coast Road does. But it may be worse because the twenty-minute ride is all uphill. After all the dreamlike descriptions I've read about Ravello, I want to enjoy the full experience without anything ruining it. *Think positive, Margie.*

One of the gems on the Amalfi Coast, Ravello is a less touristy town perched high above the Gulf of Salerno and the towns of Amalfi and Maiori. Suspended almost 1,200 feet above sea level, Ravello is one of the more sparsely inhabited towns on this coast, with a population of 2,500, although in the height of its prosperity at the end of the twelfth century, I understand Ravello had 25,000 inhabitants.

Much quieter than its busy neighbors, Positano and Amalfi, Ravello is known to be a favorite destination for artists, writers, and musicians. It has the distinction of having been home to Richard Wagner, M. C. Escher, Gore Vidal, Virginia Woolf, Sara Teasdale, Henrik Ibsen, and Giovanni Boccaccio. Celebrities like Andy Warhol, Mick Jagger, Greta

Garbo, and Paul Newman have become enamored by its charm.

From its vantage point high above the sea, Ravello provides some of the most picturesque views of the Amalfi Coast. After making his home here for years, Gore Vidal once said, "Twenty-five years ago I was asked by an American magazine what was the most beautiful place that I had ever seen in all my travels, and I said the view from the belvedere of the Villa Cimbrone on a bright winter's day when the sky and the sea were each so vividly blue that it was not possible to tell one from the other."

Famous composer Richard Wagner found his inspiration in Ravello during the late nineteenth century. Because of Wagner's influence, music is a major part of the DNA of this town, which boasts a vibrant cultural scene. Ravello prides itself on being known as *la città della musica*, the City of Music. Celebrating more than sixty years, the Wagner Summer Festival takes place between April and October at Villa Rufolo, on a stage overlooking the sea Also known as the Ravello Festival, this summer-long event retains the distinction of being one of the most renowned and oldest festivals in Italy.

Various esteemed symphony orchestras have played here over the past half century, including the Royal Philharmonic and London Symphony Orchestra, and a plethora of famous jazz musicians, actors, composers, singers, opera singers, and dancers have performed. I'd love to be here one time for a nighttime open-air concert under the light of a full moon.

Since it's daytime, I'm content to wander around the tiny alleys and discover hidden doorways and historical churches. A few minutes into my walk through town, I notice a young man driving a pint-sized vehicle that looks like a golf cart with a box built onto the back. What intrigues me is what he's transporting. Inside the vehicle is a crystal chandelier, not protected in any way, but rather positioned sideways in the cargo area, and it appears to take up the entire space. He drives up a hill that is only wide enough for his little truck with inches to spare. His vehicle trudges along at the slowest possible speed, and he stops to inspect his precious cargo at least three separate times. *Only in Italy*, I remind myself, and smile. Ravello is the perfect place to put into practice *il dolce far niente*, the sweetness of doing nothing. Here, I can immerse myself in the atmosphere of tranquility.

In the heart of Ravello, in the main square known as Piazza Vescovado, is the Duomo, an eleventh-century church initially dedicated to Our Lady of the Assumption and later consecrated to San Pantaleone, patron saint of Ravello. One of its most interesting features is its thirteenth-century bell tower, along with its bronze doors made up of fifty-four rectangular panels depicting the life of Christ. As recently as 1973, a full restoration of the cathedral was completed.

I'd like to see the interior of this cathedral, but the people sitting on the entrance steps are more interesting at the moment. Clad in brightly colored cycling jerseys, bike shorts, and helmets, sixteen men pose for a photo while another cyclist takes the picture. I bet my exercise-fanatic brother Rick would like to be here to exchange stories with these guys. He rides with a bike club in the States and likes the camaraderie as well as the exercise. Thinking back to my winding bus ride up the hill to Ravello, I don't even want to imagine the grueling challenge these cyclists faced in order to reach these hilltop towns. I'm convinced they're happy for a chance to take a break in the center of Ravello.

Near the piazza are a few shops, including a jewelry store, a ceramic shop, and a mini market with a basket of lemons outside its door. The giant pieces of citrus look as if they just came off a tree, since the leaves are still attached. A few people are casually strolling, and there's no evidence of shopping frenzy here, a stark difference from the crowded streets in Positano and Sorrento. Restaurants and B&Bs are close by but blend into the fabric of this quiet place. The environment seems relaxed; not a single person appears to be in a hurry—tourists and local alike. Shop owners take time to have conversations with passersby. Ravello seems subdued, and the tourists almost appear to be in a state of suspended animation. I like it, and I'm happy to have a flexible agenda.

A poster in both English and Italian advertising a Ravello Sense Ticket catches my attention: "One ticket for all sites of Ravello." This deal sounds good to me, since it includes entrance to the cathedral, a small cathedral museum, Villa Rufolo, and Villa Cimbrone.

The ticket is sold only inside the cathedral, so I make my way there to purchase this all-in-one voucher. I find myself inside the museum, which is a big room attached to the church. It's no surprise to me that nobody else is visiting the museum. Museums aren't my favorite places, but since this one is included in the ticket, I imagine this deserves some of my attention. Most of the displays are sculptures and works of art related to Ravello, and after ten minutes of browsing, I'm ready to see the cathedral.

Like its façade, the interior of the Ravello Cathedral is not something I'd describe as magnificent or spectacular. Like the town, it is unpretentious. I slip into one of the wooden pews and kneel down as I take a moment or two to pray, like I usually do when I enter a church in Italy. As I glance around,

I find some of the cathedral's features compelling, especially the mosaics. Six ornate, spiral columns decorated in mosaics support a colossal pulpit. Each column sits on the back of a sculptured lion. This thirteenth-century Pulpit of the Gospels is the work of Nicolo di Bartolomeo. I'm glad I didn't miss this.

***

Two of the main attractions in Ravello are ancient villas that I have only seen from the outside on a previous trip, so today is a good time to explore them more thoroughly. My choice is to do them at my leisure, by way of self-guided walks. Somewhat secluded, Villa Cimbrone is a ten-minute walk from the main square and accessible only on foot. On the way, I walk past some interesting places and stop to check them out. A creative, attention-grabbing sign makes me smile: "Save Water - Drink Limoncello." Very appropriate.

Originally an eleventh-century patrician villa, Villa Cimbrone sits on fifteen acres, much more expansive than my preconceived notions, and is surrounded by gardens, gazebos, statues, and fountains. After a couple of hours, my exercise level is surpassing its norm, gauging by the amount of walking here. *Rick, I hope you're smiling as you read this.*

After a total remodeling in the early twentieth century, Villa Cimbrone is a luxury five-star hotel today, with a price tag to match, but its magnificent gardens are open to the public. The first thing to see inside the gardens is the crypt, and its architectural style is impressive.

I learn that this Gothic open gallery is often used for wedding receptions, and the space is patterned after Fountains Abbey in Yorkshire, England. Its design appears medieval, yet its construction is early twentieth century. I am inspired by the symmetry and perfection of the columns' positions. An architecture student would fall in love with this place on the spot. The silence at the crypt allows me to contemplate the moment and take pleasure in the grace that surrounds me. The fact that I am alone here makes the experience even more surreal.

Soon I enter a long walkway, a wide, pergola-shaded dirt path aptly named the Avenue of Immensity, and at the end is a statue of Ceres. I'm happy I didn't miss this beautiful walk. Some of the paths consist of wide, uneven steps with railings crafted from tree limbs, all very natural. The undisturbed atmosphere here is inspiring, so peaceful, the antithesis to the noise and busyness of the tourist towns of this coast. A stroll through the gardens here rejuvenates my soul and relaxes my body.

Continuing to walk, I arrive at the famous Terrace of Infinity. A popular venue for destination weddings because the views are superb, Villa Cimbrone is probably best known for this outdoor terrace, also called the Belvedere of Infinity. Lined with sculptured marble Roman busts, the views of the Tyrrhenian Sea and coastline below are unsurpassed. Quite a few tourists pose for photos here, and since my preference is to shoot nature photographs sans people, I have to wait to capture the perfect image without tourists in the shot. The spectacular views of the coastline make the uphill walking and numerous steps and staircases worth the effort. I could stay here for an hour or more.

***

By now, my stomach hints that it's time for lunch, and I head back toward the Duomo and a favorite restaurant that I recall being recommended by a tour guide. La Vecchia Cantina comes into view, and I find it an ideal place to satisfy my hunger cravings. This family-run restaurant serves excellent meals at reasonable prices. One of their specialties is pasta with marinara sauce and pumpkin, which I'm told by another patron is delicious. My choice is pasta *arrabbiata* and a salad of tomatoes and arugula, which is not only tasty but healthy. I don't linger too long here, since I want to visit Villa Rufolo before I have to say arrivederci to Ravello.

Not far from the restaurant, I notice a sign pointing to a shop with an intriguing name, and curiosity persuades me to go inside. With a store called Wine and Drugs, I have to see for myself whether drugs are really sold here and, if so, exactly what kind. I recall hearing that marijuana is legal in small amounts in Italy, but I don't know if that's true or just a story. Things can be different sometimes in Italy, and I want to know. After a brief conversation and a few laughs with the friendly saleswomen, I understand this is a shop specializing in wine, organic olive oil, grappa, and a few other food items. I have my answer: no illegal drugs are sold here.

Situated a few hundred feet from the main square is Villa Rufolo, a thirteenth-century building which today is a museum, complemented by its magnificent designed and manicured gardens. It's also the home of the Ravello Music Festival. As I follow the stone corridor to its entrance, the fragrant aroma of the perfectly placed red and white flowers lining the path permeates the air, and I take some time to savor the moment. The scent, combined with the visual, is so appealing that I almost want to stay outside and not even check out anything else. But I acquiesce to reason and enter through an arched opening in an old stone tower. As I walk along an inner pathway, I soon reach the Moorish Cloister. As a photographer, I'm intrigued by the open arched room, with its colonnade of thirty-six polished arches, that depicts an exceptional Arab-Sicilian architectural style. I can envision a fairy-tale wedding reception in this amazing space.

Villa Rufolo lays claim to two towers, and the largest is Torre Maggiore, a Moorish tower that rises almost one hundred feet into the sky. The villa's castle-like appearance still fascinates me, despite the fact that what was once a luxurious interior is only a memory today.

The gardens are exquisite, and two separate terraces comprise the property. I'm overtaken by the scent of the natural flora as I stroll amid the containers of colorful flowers which have been arranged in intricate geometric patterns. The edge of the terrace hangs out over the waters of the Tyrrhenian Sea, and I can only describe the view as orgasmic. Now I understand why Wagner was inspired to complete the second act of his opera *Parsifal* here, and why the summer concert series takes place in this fabulous location with this breathtaking backdrop.

As if this isn't enough, a steep set of stairs takes me to a higher terrace, and I'm grateful I don't have knee or hip problems that would prevent me from climbing up to appreciate the breathtaking view from an even higher elevation. I thank God that I also don't have any vertigo or dizziness issues. I know I am fortunate to be able to travel and enjoy beautiful places such as this, and I appreciate every moment I'm given to do so.

As my ninety-nine-year-old aunt advised me before she passed away, "Go to Italy now, while you're healthy, while you can walk up all those hills and steps, because one day you won't be able to go anymore." Wise advice from someone who did go to Italy while she was able. These are words I will always remember. Thanks so much, Auntie Buzz.

On the SITA bus back to Amalfi, down those same zigzagging roads, my mind is filled with memories of the events of this special day spent alone in Ravello. Most tourists never take the opportunity to travel off the beaten path to under-the-radar destinations like Ravello. The Amalfi Coast is filled with quaint, out-of-the-way hamlets, villages, and towns in the hills above the sea. The bus makes a few local stops on the return trip to drop off passengers after their workdays have ended. Names like Castiglione, Pontone, Minuta, and San Pietro are new for me, but Scala is the one town I've heard of before. I think maybe I'll add this to my bucket list for the next trip here. What I know about Scala is that it's the oldest village on the Amalfi Coast, and from my research I recall that every October at harvest time, Festa della Castagna (the Chestnut Festival) occurs. An entire weekend of entertainment, music, games, and all varieties of food — made with chestnuts, of course. Sounds like fun.

After twenty minutes on the bus, I'm back to the busier lifestyle of Amalfi, where I'm staying for a few nights. While I appreciate the serenity of Ravello, I also like the excitement of Amalfi. Let the evening begin!

Transportation Options

Italy's public transportation suffices in most locations, but not necessarily in all places. And believe it or not, some Italian communities do not have a train station. This is true of all the towns on the Amalfi Coast. Surprised to hear this? The closest thing is the Circumvesuviana commuter train that runs from Sorrento to the villages and towns along the Sorrentine peninsula and around Mount Vesuvius. The nearest city with train connections is Salerno, which is at the southern end of the Amalfi Coast but not technically part of it.

Over forty trains a day arrive in Salerno from Naples, including the high-speed trains of Italo and Trenitalia. The forty-six-kilometer trip takes thirty-five or forty minutes, and the cost of a one-way ticket is between five and fifteen euros. Both of these train companies have websites in English and Italian, and advance booking can be made online, at kiosks in Italian train stations, or from a smartphone.

When I plan my travels, I prefer to book online in advance whenever my dates are confirmed, and both train companies offer amazing discounts and special promotions much of the time. For instance, Trenitalia may feature two tickets for the price of one on Saturdays, discounts for same-day return travel, and group discounts when two to five tickets for the same trip are purchased together. Italo services fewer cities in Italy, although they seem to continually add more locations. Some of the offers they highlight include a forty percent senior discount for those sixty and over, though it isn't valid on Fridays, Saturdays, and Sundays. Another promotion with savings up to fifty percent is for same-day return trips.

I rate my experiences on both Italo's and Trenitalia's high-speed trains as A-plus. If I'm traveling between major cities, I try to book an Italo train or a Trenitalia Frecce train as my first choice. Direct routes and speed guarantee the fastest trip, barring any unforeseen circumstances. The Trenitalia Frecciarossa trains provide connections from Naples to Salerno and can reach speeds as high as 360 km/hr. Known for combining high speed with maximum comfort, these trains all have air-conditioning, Wi-Fi, power outlets at each seat, ample luggage space, LED lighting, wheelchair accessibility, and restrooms in every coach. The newest Frecciarossa 1000 is capable of achieving speeds of 400 km/hr. Italo Treno's high-speed trains are all equipped with reclining leather seats, power sockets, Wi-Fi, and plenty of luggage space. Onboard vending machines are available for snacks and beverages. The newest additions, their Italo Pendolino trains, can attain maximum speeds of 250 km/hr.

*****

Once in Salerno or Naples, the process of reaching the Amalfi Coast still needs to be arranged via one of the three viable transportation options. Salerno is the southern hub for transport to the Amalfi Coast. With a population of 133,000, this city is much larger than any of the coastal towns. From Salerno, transportation options to the Amalfi Coast are by bus, boat, or car.

SITA buses leave from the Salerno train station and travel to the cities on the Amalfi Coast. The end of the route is Amalfi, another transportation hub, and the ride takes an hour and fifteen minutes and costs €3.40. For travel beyond Amalfi, to Positano or all the way to Sorrento, the ticket price from Salerno is €6.80 and involves a transfer to another bus in Amalfi. As of this writing, a new twenty-four-hour ticket, which allows an unlimited number of trips, is available at a cost of €10. The beneficial feature of this ticket is that it includes bus trips to cities above the Amalfi Coast Road as well. These tickets are not sold on the buses but can be purchased in the *tabaccheria* (cigarette shops) and also at newspaper stands, bars, and cafés. I remember a time when I boarded the bus in Salerno, expecting to buy the ticket from the bus driver. He politely informed me in Italian that I needed to purchase it at the *tabaccheria* inside the train station, and he was nice enough to wait for me. A little added stress I didn't need, but at least he waited, and I learned a valuable lesson.

These buses can be crowded, especially during the months of June, July, and August. Sometimes, standing room only reigns, and with luggage the trip becomes more challenging. Trust me, I've been there. Depending on one's budget, the best option for a no-stress trip, especially during the high season, is to make a reservation with a private car service. Whenever I travel to Positano from Naples these days, I book a private transfer company. More on that later in this chapter.

As a port city, Salerno provides ferry service to the Amalfi Coast, as well as to Capri, from different ferry companies. The ferries to Capri operate from May to October, and those to the Amalfi Coast between April and October. The trip between Salerno and Amalfi can be as short as thirty-five minutes or as long as seventy minutes if it includes stops in the towns along the way. Prices range between eight and twelve euros.

For me, one of the benefits of taking the ferry is experiencing this coastline from the perspective of the water. As the first of the towns comes into view, a surge of adrenaline courses through me, and I can hardly contain my sense of excitement. Like a postcard, Vietri sul Mare is in full view, from the sea all the way up the mountain. I try to imagine a fisherman near the marina dragging his catch up those hills at the end of his workday. More little towns appear as I get closer to my destination, and I make a mental note to visit these fishing villages, like Cetara and Furore. As the ferry nears Amalfi, I'm delighted to capture the scenes with the camera on my iPhone. The ferry captain steers his watercraft close to the pier so he can drop off and pick up passengers here, providing me with even more time for photos from various angles. I'm loving it.

Another advantage the ferry provides over the SITA bus is the lack of need to disembark at Amalfi when Positano is the destination, and this can be an important consideration when travel planning. One of the disadvantages of ferry travel is the timetable. The ferry schedule provides less departure and return choices than does the bus. And, of course, the season dictates whether the ferries are even in service.

***

I find it's good to have more than one available travel option in Italy because situations like transportation strikes can happen, or a flight can be delayed, forcing a missed connection. I know this from personal experience on a travel day gone wrong. I've learned that when I travel to towns in southern Italy I can expect an adventure, particularly if the travel is by train.

Today is no exception. The year is 2014, and I'm traveling from Colle d'Anchise, the tiny village where my grandfather was born, in the region of Molise. My cousin Antonella drops me off at the train station in the nearby town of Boiano, thirty minutes early.

We hug and kiss as we say goodbye, and she's barely out of sight when a train official approaches and asks me where I'm going. "Salerno," I reply. Without uttering a word, he directs me to follow him, and points to a waiting bus, already filled with people.

Confused at first, I soon learn that the 1:45 p.m. train to Salerno has some problem, and this bus is transporting all of the passengers that were supposed to be on the train to the town of Isernia. From there, I'm told, the plan is to board a train to Caserta. I assume that once I reach Caserta, I will be able to transfer to another train headed for Salerno. The cramped conditions and the sudden change in travel plans make for a stressful bus trip for me.

Once the bus arrives in Isernia, I'm unsure of what's going on but follow the crowd as we walk about five hundred meters in the rain to the train station. I'm grateful that I understand enough Italian and can communicate with other passengers, who help me determine which track will have the train going to my destination. But if I'm honest with myself,

I'm somewhat nervous. As one who likes to plan and have everything run smoothly, I tend to lack patience and tolerance in these kinds of circumstances.

Once I'm seated in the train car, a kind, young Italian man from Napoli helps me by lifting up my bag to store on the overhead rack. I thank him in Italian. "Grazie, Signore. Lo apprezzo." He tells me he is a *pizzaiolo* (pizza maker) in Posillipo near Napoli. When I tell him I've been to Naples and show him some of my photos, he smiles and seems impressed.

This train is not overly crowded, and an older woman seated across from me smiles as she acknowledges my presence. She appears friendly, and I strike up a conversation in what Italian I know, explaining where I'm from and where I'm headed. "Sono Americana. Vado a Salerno," I say to her. She informs me that this train is going to Caserta and is helpful in explaining in Italian that I need to get off there and change trains to go to Salerno. I thank her—"Grazie mille, Signora"—grateful for her help.

At 3:05 p.m. the train departs from the Isernia station. The trip to Caserta is supposed to take an hour and a half, but not today. Since life can run in slow motion in Italy, this train is delayed at Venafro for some unknown reason. For the next twenty-five minutes, the train sits on the tracks with no train personnel in sight. Nobody gets on or off, and the doors remain closed. Forget about any overhead announcements—which I'd welcome, even in Italian.

Even though I'm irritated and nervous, I've learned from my travels that it's important to be flexible, because these instances occur more often than not in Italy and are completely beyond my control. I tell myself not to worry about it or get stressed out; instead, I use the time to write my blog post and edit photos on my iPad. This is Italy, and you have to take the good with the bad. It's the whole package or nothing.

In due course, the train begins to move, and we pull into the Caserta station a few minutes before five o'clock. I overhear some of the men in my compartment discussing my predicament. They express concern to each other about the possibility that I might miss the last train to Salerno today, since the arrival in Caserta is seventy minutes later than scheduled. One man, who speaks some English, informs me that there had been a crash early this morning near Boiano, hence the lengthy delay. *How kind of him to be concerned for me,* I think. We then engage in a conversation, partly in English but mostly in Italian, about how common these problems are in the south of Italy. One of the men states that they need to have a revolution. You gotta love the passion.

As I stand up in preparation to get off this train, the attractive young pizza maker from Napoli offers to carry my bag. *How gentlemanly of him.* "Arrivederci. Buona serata," I say, expressing my thanks for his kindness and wishing him a good evening.

The kind woman seated across from me smiles. "Buon viaggio," she says, wishing me safe travels as she kisses me on both cheeks. She tells me that next time I come here I must stay at her house. I don't know where I've met friendlier people than in Italy. Grazie mille a tutti!

As I walk down the platform, I ponder how no one ever checked my train ticket during this entire ordeal. I still can't figure out what criteria determine whose tickets get checked and whose don't. More often than not in the south of Italy, and especially on these regional trains, tickets never get checked. It seems to be a hit-or-miss situation. I guess it's the honor system here.

Once inside the station, I stand in line to talk to a man at the ticket desk, and he informs me that the next train to Salerno leaves at 6:12 p.m. I remember taking this same train three years ago when my train was diverted here, so no problem. The SITA buses run well into the evening, so I'm relieved knowing I'll arrive in Amalfi sometime tonight. I'm not too worried, as I believe this is all part of the adventure.

Thirty minutes prior to my scheduled departure time, I check the overhead sign to locate which track my train is on — *Binario 5* — as well as what other stops it will make and its estimated arrival time in Salerno. Just to double-check, I decide to ask the train official who happens to be walking nearby, and he verifies the information. This is great news. I board this larger and more modern train with ease, delighted to find the doorway is level with the platform. With no steps to climb, it's much easier to haul my luggage onto the train.

It's the little things in life that make a big difference. Since the car is empty, I have my choice of seats, and I opt for the first row, where there is plenty of space for my bag on the floor next to me. As I settle in for the ride, I breathe a sigh of relief. As always, everything is working out fine. During the relaxing trip, a Trenitalia official appears, and, to my disbelief, he actually checks my ticket and punches it with an old-fashioned hole punch. You just never know.

On the ride, I have time to think and anticipate that if luck is on my side, I'll be able to buy a bus ticket at the station and catch the next bus to Amalfi without having to wait too long.

I guess I'm hoping for too much, because if I think this trip to Amalfi could continue without any more problems,

I'm mistaken. The train arrives in Salerno at exactly 7:15 p.m., and I rush downstairs to the *edicola* (newsstand) to buy the one-way SITA bus ticket for €3.40. Familiar with the station and bus area, I walk outside toward the bus stop only to find the familiar blue SITA bus dark, the bus doors closed, and no driver in sight. "What's this? Why isn't the bus ready to go?" I ask myself as I start to panic.

Wondering whether the bus stop may have been relocated, I approach a young man, who looks to be the age of a college student, and ask him if he knows where the bus is. "Dov'è la fermata dell'autobus?" I say, waving my hand in the direction of the bus stop. Grateful that he understands my limited Italian, I learn from him that either a riot or a strike occurred earlier today, and all buses are out of service. *You've got to be kidding me!* By now my patience is wearing thin, after traveling for the last six hours. But this wonderful young man, God bless him, takes the time to direct me to the office inside the station, and he tells me the woman will help me. "Grazie mille," I say, and walk inside, flustered but grateful.

The pleasant female employee makes eye contact with me, and she stops what she's doing. She must be able to discern the frantic look on my face, and she is willing to listen to my story. "Un autobus arriverà tra dieci minuti, alle 7:30 del pomeriggio. Non ti preoccupare," she says, telling me not to worry and assuring me that a bus will indeed be coming in ten minutes. My luck seems to have changed after all. I go back outside and walk toward the bus stop. Right on time, a big SITA bus appears in its normal parking area, lights on and a bus driver in his seat. Within three minutes or less, I board with my bag and I'm on my way to Amalfi, my final destination for today. I have the next four nights to relax in my hotel with a view, and I'm definitely looking forward to it.

***

After this adventurous travel day, I can understand why a car is helpful in southern Italy. These locations are not so easy to reach, and relying on public transportation can be like planning a beach day during the rainy season. Having a plan B is always a good idea.

So, the third option, using a car as the transportation of choice, can include driving a rental car or hiring a private driver. I've done both, and each has its pros and cons, but when I'm traveling solo, the cost to rent a vehicle can be prohibitive. In the Campania region of Italy, several reliable car companies provide excellent service, and my experiences with them are nothing less than first-rate. I think the benefits outweigh the costs in most instances, and not only does the decision to hire a private service reduce stress, but it also provides peace of mind with the assurance that travel arrangements are secured.

I also appreciate the added benefit of meeting a local person who is fluent in Italian and English. Aside from practicing my Italian, a one-on-one conversation with the driver opens a window into the real Italian lifestyle. My most recent experience is with Drive Amalfi, a private car service that arranges private shore excursions, tours, and transfers. Communication through email with Salvatore Lucibello, the owner, is efficient, and the drivers are prompt. Of the four times I've used this company, my rating remains excellent. I especially remember Nicola and Francesco, both friendly, professional drivers with terrific personalities, as our conversations included a diverse variety of interesting subjects.

Another private car service I've used and highly recommend is Pleasant Travel, owned and operated by Mariano Fiorentino, the generous and happy Italian man who treated my group to fresh mozzarella in Piano di Sorrento. His drivers and guides are not only efficient and reliable, but also pleasant, friendly, and fluent in English. His company features the ability to customize a trip, which I did when making arrangements for an all-day tour with them.

Whichever transportation option works best, getting around the Amalfi Coast may be a process but is well worth the effort, and I'll return every time I have the chance.

Musings

Diverse landscapes like rugged precipices, terraced vineyards, steep staircases, and pebbled beaches comprise the Unesco World Heritage site of Costiera Amalfitana. The sheer beauty of this heaven on Earth is enough to make any human being fall in love with the Amalfi Coast. Every town reaching into the Tyrrhenian Sea mirrors a perfect postcard engraved in my mind forever. I believe the Amalfi Coast personifies the most beautiful place on the planet.

What attracts me from four thousand miles away with such a strong magnetic force transcends the sheer beauty of the Amalfi Coast. When I'm home, I dream of this place and wish I could be here. What is the allure? The answer can be complicated because like any love affair, mine with the Amalfi Coast has no concrete explanation, nor does it need one. I just know the appeal prevails, and when I'm on this coast of Italy, I'm happy, inspired, and feel at home.

Whenever I walk the countless steps and twisting uphill paths that are so much a part of this landscape, I contemplate the people who live here. These staircases and climbs are part of everyday life for them. I admire how they take it in stride without complaining. Even the elderly Italians, people in their eighties, walk up these hills on a daily basis as they drag grocery carts behind them. I remember Crescenzo, a robust, gray-haired, seventy-three-year-old gentleman who had to turn around and wait for me, twenty stairs below him, while I paused to catch my breath.

On my first day in a new place, I like to familiarize myself with the layout of each town, an undertaking that can be challenging, but in a good way. Like the arms of an octopus, streets and alleys branch away from the main piazza in numerous directions, and not in geometric order. What I prefer most when exploring is to meander away from the center of town on one of these backstreets with no itinerary or plan.

I never worry about losing my way, because the Amalfi Coast towns are not that big, and most of them reach the sea sooner or later. Italians are happy to help when a tourist is lost, and I know how to ask for directions in Italian. A simple "Dov'è" (where is . . .?) followed by "per favore" (please) works wonders. In most instances, Italians are not only pleasant and eager to give directions, but they will go out of their way to provide adequate guidance. On more than one occasion, I recall a shop owner leaving their shop and walking two blocks down the street with me until we reach a corner. Then with a wave of both hands, they point in the direction I need to go. No matter how far away something might be, to an Italian the distance is always five hundred meters and straight down the road: "Cinquecento metri diritto, diritto." And most everything is only "cinque minuti" (five minutes) away. I love the Italian people.

Whether I'm at home or in Italy, a beach is near and dear to my heart. The Amalfi Coast beaches are not soft and sandy.

Instead, the sand is a gray color and full of pebbles, to the point that I need sandals or shoes to walk on the gravelly shoreline without hurting my feet. Packed with bodies in summertime, the beaches appear as a palette of colorful umbrellas, blue and white in Maiori, orange and green in Positano. In any season the seashore calls my name, and the cerulean water mesmerizes me.

In 2016, after spending two weeks in the beachfront Hotel Pupetto, I awaken to a sound unlike the quiet waves reaching the shore. Noisy banging prompts me to walk onto my balcony to investigate the source of this uproar. An army of human ants work by hand, dragging boats onto the shore and removing wooden planks, one at a time, from walkways across the sand. Curiosity prompts me to explore the reasons for this activity, and I am compelled to see for myself up close, so I dress and sprint down the stairs to the first floor lobby. "Gabriella, what's happening outside? I hear a lot of noise," I say. By now I've become friends with the pleasant young woman with the pixie-style haircut and fashionable scarf around her neck. The granddaughter of the original owner of this hotel, she remains an integral member of the Pupetto family and manages the front desk. Gabriella smiles as she explains, "Yes, every year at the end of the season, all the beach concessions must come down and be stored for winter. It's the law." She tells me this in a matter-of-fact tone, and I look at her in disbelief.

"What? You mean they have to dismantle their entire beach bar — the walls and the kitchen and all?"

"That's right. It's a lot of work, and they do it every year at this time, mid-October. And then in the spring they have to rebuild it all. My brother is out at the bar working now to take everything apart. They are used to it. It's important

77

because the strong winter winds and storms will push the sea over the shoreline and destroy everything."

The idea of disassembling everything only to have to reassemble it six months from now seems incredible to me, yet I know Gabriella is telling me the truth about how rugged the lifestyle can be on the Amalfi Coast.

"Wow, thank you, Gabriella. I had no idea. I think I'll go and have a look myself." I walk outside and make my way to my favorite beach bar next door, Da Ferdinando. Just like she told me, the waiters and bartenders, cooks, and even Guido, the owner, work together as they reposition boats and dismantle the outdoor restaurant and bar. Half of the blue wooden tables and chairs are already folded, ready for storage. The kitchen is almost nonexistent now, although their signature sign still hangs in full view. A smile emerges on my face as I read it: "Life's too short to drink cheap wine." I wave at Guido, and he nods back and smiles as he works with his crew to get one of the boats as close as possible to the storage area. I'm going to miss this place, but I plan to return sometime soon. I'm still in shock to learn of this yearly ritual when the beach transforms into a silent, ghostly place.

***

Since this coast is rocky and mountainous, its highest point almost a mile above sea level, navigating on foot can be challenging. When hiking in the higher elevations, a few miles may take hours, especially because the paths wind around the mountainside, and straight up or down routes do not exist. I may have to climb twenty stairs up, walk twenty feet, and then climb down ten mores stairs to reach a particular point.

The distance from one location to another may be a mile as the crow flies but three miles by the only available footpath. The lifestyle on this coast appears simple, and the local people spend the majority of their time in their own towns unless they work in another coastal town. For example, the distance in a straight line on a map between Naples and Amalfi is only twenty-three miles. By car, along the shortest route, this increases to forty miles, and travel time is an hour and twenty minutes. A lot of travelers make the huge mistake of thinking they can travel all over the Amalfi Coast in a short time. I understand from the past ten years of traveling here that nothing occurs fast in Italy, and the amount of time one thinks something may take is most always undercalculated.

Although I appreciate that Positano may quite possibly be the most breathtaking location in Italy, I also realize it's not the best choice as a base for travel to Sorrento or an island like Procida, off the coast of Napoli. For the second time now, I'm trying to figure a way to make a day trip to Procida from Positano, and as much as I hate to admit it, I realize this reality remains next to impossible. To attempt this fairy-tale scenario would be a logistical nightmare and, at most, might allow two hours of time to explore Procida. What a waste that would be, since an island like Procida deserves much more time. So, I give up the notion—for now. On a future trip I will have to make a decision to stay in Naples a few days; from there, a ferry ride to Procida is not only doable, but efficient, and should allow enough time to uncover some of its magic. All part of the travel planning process.

Whenever I visit this *bel paese* (beautiful country), my interest leans in the direction of the people. A place can be the epitome of loveliness, and much of the Amalfi Coast meets this portrayal, yet the people fascinate me most of all.

Curiosity about their way of life prompts me to strike up a conversation whenever the occasion arises. Common traits I detect are a clear sense of pride in their heritage and a fierce resiliency. Maybe more than these two characteristics is their eagerness to share their stories with anyone who exhibits the slightest interest.

Today is a warm fall day in Amalfi, and I'm traveling alone. As I wander up the main street, I discover narrow alleys and side streets with restaurants, ceramic shops, and businesses the locals frequent, like a barbershop, a laundry and a supermarket. The more I walk, the higher the elevation, and although I'm far from being physically fit, at least I'm in better shape than the last time I came to Italy. The walking on inclined streets doesn't bother me, which is good since I intend to walk a lot while here to balance out my caloric intake.

I turn onto a side road and ask a local man who's walking toward me if he knows what the view is like farther up. He explains in English that more homes are up this hill, not the panoramic view that I'm hoping to find. "Grazie, Signore," I reply as I turn around and retrace my steps back to Via Lorenzo d'Amalfi, the main street in Amalfi. He continues his walk alongside me, and we resume our verbal exchange, which turns out to be a history lesson for me. I would have loved to learn history in this manner when I was in elementary school, instead of reading about it in boring textbooks from which I gained no understanding of World History.

"Mi chiama Margherita. Sono Americana," I say, delighted to practice my foreign language skills.

The man pauses, looks into my eyes, and says that he is pleased to meet me. "Piacere. I am Antonio." He appears to be in his seventies, and I learn that he is retired. Wearing a white cap and dressed in an oversized, light-blue polo shirt, navy blue shorts, and blue beach sandals, this clean-shaven man with short, white hair begins to tell me a story. He explains to me that the road on which we are now walking did not exist at one time, because a river had been there and bridges were built. I don't know how long ago this might have been, but I'm intrigued by his story.

By the time we reach the main square, Piazza del Duomo, Antonio expands on his story, informing me that the sea had once come all the way up to the location of St Andrew's Cathedral. We walk a bit more and he pauses, looking high above the cathedral and into the mountains above Amalfi, and points to a grayish stone tower. I had noticed it earlier and wondered about its history. He tells me that this is Torre dello Ziro and describes the legend about a princess who died in the tower. Fascinated, I want to hear more, but that's all he shares.

Later, I learn that the watchtower dates back to 1480, when it was constructed over ruins of a twelfth-century tower. The tower's legend begins with another Antonio, Duke Antonio Piccolomini, who ruled Amalfi, a powerful and wealthy feudal duchy. When Antonio died in 1493, his son Alfonso assumed control as Duke of Amalfi. A few years prior, Alfonso married Giovanna d'Aragona, daughter of the half-brother of King Frederick of Naples. Young Alfonso died at an early age, leaving Giovanna a widow before her second son was born. She ruled Amalfi but fell in love with a butler, another Antonio, and they married in a secret ceremony. Maintaining secrecy for years regarding their marriage and the three additional children they had together was eventually Giovanna's downfall. When her brothers discovered the story, they accused her of betrayal of love. Her husband, Antonio, fled to Milan, where he was captured and killed. Giovanna was captured along with her children, and they were forced to live in the tower as hostages until all of them were killed there. Some *Amalfitani* believe they can hear her ghost crying as they pass by the tower.

A number of stories about what really happened persist to this day, but this seems to be the most popular version. I find it spellbinding. Legends are alive on the Amalfi Coast, and any native from here knows them all and is more than happy to impart a tale to anyone willing to listen.

Aside from the imposing architectural landmark of the cathedral, an interesting baroque-style fountain graces Piazza del Duomo. The Fountain of Saint Andrew, carved in 1760, features a marble sculpture of the patron saint of Amalfi on the top. Not only does this fountain pay homage to an apostle, but it also includes nymphs and cherubs, which seems appropriate, given the heavenly theme. What is even more unique, and perhaps the reason tourists often photograph this otherwise-commonplace fountain, is a figure of a woman. She holds her breasts in her hands, and drinking water flows freely from her nipples. I wonder if the erotic nature of the sculpture is the reason the fountain that once sat at the foot of the stairs to the cathedral was moved to this location in the early twentieth century. No big surprise that Antonio poses for me to take his picture in front of the sculpture.

My unanticipated conversation with this Amalfi man replaces anything I can read in a guidebook, because he teaches me about the local culture and history. "Amalfi had been one of four republics prior to the Unification of Italy. It was quite powerful as the Maritime Republic of all of southern Italy," he declares with pride. What I think I will remember most was what he shares about the Amalfi people. "When they die, they know they will go to Paradise, and they already live in Paradise." An interesting and comforting belief.

After all this time, I start making my way toward Piazza Flavia Gioia and the Arsenale, a civic and naval museum close to the sea. Not willing to say goodbye yet, Antonio invites me to visit the cathedral and offers to serve as a guide. He tempts me with the additional information that a prison was once located beneath this church. "Grazie, Antonio, but I do have to leave. I will visit it another time," I say, wishing to make a quick exit before he gets other ideas.

"Okay, but when you come again, I will show you everything," Antonio promises in a flirtatious way. I'm getting used to the sexy ways of Italian men, no matter their age. As I walk away from the piazza and through the arched tunnel toward the seafront, I have to admit Antonio's attentions flattered me.

Path of the Gods Hike

I am not a hiker. Anyone who has read my tales of walking up inclines and trails in Italy knows this. I recall writing in detail about my painful ordeal in Cinque Terre in my first book, *Memoirs of a Solo Traveler – My Love Affair with Italy*. That said, I am fascinated by panoramic vistas such as those along the Path of the Gods, a trail high above the Amalfi Coast. Also known as Il Sentiero degli Dei, this footpath provides magnificent vistas from more than fifteen hundred feet overlooking the Amalfi Coast.

I must admit the thought of walking the Path of the Gods has been in the back of my mind from the time I first learned about this experience a few years ago. I wonder how demanding this hike would be. Initially dismissing the idea as being out of reach, my curiosity increases as I read more about it and see photos of the incredible views from high above the Amalfi Coast, and I'm inclined to go for it. Since I embrace a healthier lifestyle now, at least I can say that I'm in much better shape and more agile than when I hiked the Cinque Terre trail, but I'm still unsure if I'll do it or not.

In early October of 2016, the idea becomes a reality when I'm in Positano for two weeks to write without distractions. I decide this hike will be one of only two excursions I allow myself during my two-week retreat. Once I commit to this challenge, I'm happy about my decision and look forward to the adventure. My plan is to take a bus to the starting point in Bomerano and follow the trail to Nocelle, a tiny village high above Positano. From my research I understand that two return options exist—either a bus back to Positano or a climb down 1500 steps. (Yes, you read that correctly: 1500.)

When the bus arrives in the hamlet of Bomerano in Agerola, a group of eight hikers, including myself, alights from the bus in a soft rain. Nobody else is in sight, and no signs point to where we need to go. We begin walking toward Piazza Paolo Capasso and locate a bar next to Hotel Gentile on the corner of Via Pennino. We enter the bar, partly to escape the drizzle and partly to grab an espresso and *cornetto* before beginning the hike. I buy a bottle of *acqua naturale*, also called still water, the noncarbonated variety. I walk outside alone, and pull my scarf up over my head to start my trek in the rain.

Just outside the bar, a large green-and-white sign points in the direction of the Path of the Gods. Information in Italian, German, and English describes where I'm about to go: "Walking time from here to Positano along the Path of the Gods - 4 hours 30 minutes, 9 km, 250 meters height difference." I understand the time to be less without walking down all the steps to Positano. As I begin my walk on a cobblestone road, a utility pole with a small, unobtrusive rectangular red-and-white marker painted at eye level attracts my attention. I remember reading that these types of signs lead the way, as I smile to myself and keep going. A few of

85

the others from the bus lag behind me at intervals, and a couple wearing red rain ponchos passes by me.

The beautifully landscaped stone path precedes the trailhead, and since I am still in the town, I walk past a resident's personal garden where I see tomatoes staked in an orderly fashion. Soon I walk down a set of stone stairs, at the end of which is a sign pointing right. "Sentiero degli Dei - Durata 180 min," it reads. Reassured that I'm on the correct path, I make a right turn and can see another set of wooden steps going up.

Climbing these, I find myself on a paved uphill road, where I soon enjoy a clear view of terraced gardens and the blue sea below. An overcast sky shows signs of improving weather conditions, as I notice a hint of blue close to the horizon and a glimpse of light. The rain lets up, so I remove my scarf, and now the cool, fresh air hits my face. I'm grateful for the solitude as I walk along and listen to the chirping of the birds. *This hike isn't so bad,* I think to myself, as the road is paved and not difficult.

On the right side of the street a covered opening appears in the rocky wall, and I smile as I see a cute three-wheeled vehicle I love parked at its entrance. The little truck is known as an "ape" and pronounced "ah-peh." It is often used in Italy to transport items in villages with steep, narrow streets, where a normal-size car could never maneuver. Adjacent to the cave-like opening in the wall, a sign painted in brown letters on a white surface greets me, encouraging me to continue along: "Benvenuti sul Sentiero degli Dei." It's a welcome sight!

On the other side of this wall is a gigantic mural hand-painted on white ceramic tiles with quotations from two famous visitors to the trailhead. The first is by Italo Calvino, an Italian journalist, whose words describe this spectacular place high above the sea. "Partendo proprio dal Sentiero degli dei da quella strada sospesa sul magico golfo delle Sirene, solcato ancora oggi dalla memoria e dal mito." (Starting out from the Path of the Gods, that road suspended over the magical gulf of the Sirens still furrowed today by memory and myth.)

The second quotation is credited to D.H. Lawrence, famous author of *Lady Chatterley's Lover*. "È questo il paesaggio che, dall'alto del Sentiero degli Dei, si apriva al nostro sguardo: è lo scenario di quell'estrema ansa della Costiera Amalfitana che guarda verso ovest, verso l'isola di Capri, quella costa ripida, afosa, con le montagne cristalline ove si abbandonano gli Dèi di oggi e si scopre di nuovo un sé perduto, mediterraneo, anteriore." (Is this the view that from on high along the Path of the Gods, opens to our sight: it is the picture of the great loop of the Amalfi coastline that looks towards the west, towards the Island of Capri, that precipitous coast, sultry, with the crystalline mountains where the gods of today are forsaken and you find a lost self again. Mediterranean, before you.)

I find it more than a coincidence that while I'm in Positano to write, I discover that famous writers also fell in love with the Path of the Gods. The simple knowledge that they preceded me here decades ago inspires me.

As I trudge forward, I catch a whiff of mint or rosemary in the air and savor the moment. Taking time to glance around, I notice quite a few grapevines, but their leaves have turned brown and no fruit remains, signs that the harvest is already over for this season. Down the mountainside, a few stone homes with red roofs dot the landscape, which is richly cantilevered with terraced vegetation. Closer to the road, an arched shrine crafted out of the rock encloses a blue and white statue of the Virgin Mary.

Every so often, I'm overtaken by a group of serious hikers wearing their sturdy hiking boots and backpacks and using their walking canes. Their pace is faster than mine, but I'm content taking my time and living in the moment. At this point, the uphill hike becomes a bit more challenging, and the surface changes to a dirt path mixed with stones. A not-too-sturdy-looking fence constructed from tree limbs and secured with pieces of wire borders the trail's edge nearest a cliff. An eye-catching sign nearby that reads "#climbwithgods" is self-explanatory. As I climb higher, the edge is completely unprotected and the drop down even steeper. I continue hiking higher and higher for another half hour without seeing anyone else.

Eventually I reach an overlook, where a wooden directional sign indicates Nocelle and Positano in one direction and Praiano in the other. Words cannot describe the breathtaking panoramic vista below me as I stand at what appears to be the highest point on the path. Nothing I've seen so far can compare to its stunning beauty. It's here that I catch up to the hiking group, as they are taking a break to also appreciate this wondrous scene. I hear several languages spoken, including Italian, German, and French. A member of this group introduces herself as Sarah, and we have a chance to chat a few minutes.

"Would you like me to take your picture?" she asks, noticing I'm traveling solo.

"Sure, that would be great. I really appreciate it. Thank you. My name is Margie. You must be American?"

"Yes, I'm Sarah, and I'm traveling with this French group. I'm from Vermont."

How sweet of her to offer to take a photo of me here. Talking to a fellow American for a few moments adds to the experience for me today. Most of the other hikers I'd come across earlier in the day were European. The group leaves to continue hiking, and I linger a bit longer to capture some shots of the landscape. I think I recognize the Li Galli islands in the distance. This archipelago of three islands sits a few miles off the coast of Positano.

Yellow wildflowers and terraced vineyards balance the rugged rocky walls so predominant during this adventure. In some areas where the path is not so clear, I notice the inconspicuous red-and-white markers hand-painted on a rock or a piece of wood to guide the way. In some spots, I'm required to traverse uneven stone steps that are barely visible in the brush. I can understand how this trail was a goat path and possibly still is. I bet the mules use it today. At one point the steps widen and are comprised mainly of dirt and stones with pieces of tree limb at the edge of each stair. Wobbly, unstable sections of cut tree limbs attempt to give the appearance of a railing, but in my opinion it's more of a hazard than anything else. Here, the trail becomes quite steep and the edge is completely exposed. Thanks to a sign, I am able to recognize the Convento di San Domenico and Praiano below. Here again I am presented with the choice of heading toward Praiano or Positano and Nocelle, and I choose Nocelle.

Not long after this, I arrive at another high point, and a weathered, wooden picnic table appears. I recognize the table from a photo posted on a blog I had read which recommended this spot as good for a break and some amazing photos. When I turn around to appreciate the 360-degree view in front of me, I decide to stay here for a while and inhale the fresh mountain air as I immerse myself in the natural beauty that surrounds me. Awe does not adequately describe what I'm experiencing, as I can see as far as Capri. This striking view stirs something within me that is nothing short of incredible. As a photographer, I'm composing the next ten images in my mind, yet no digital photo will replace this moment in time. I'm relishing every second here.

After walking another fifteen minutes or so, my first glimpse of Positano appears below, and I realize even more how much I value this experience. Sheer beauty prevails as the steep, rocky cliffs of the Amalfi Coast meet the undulating waters of the Mediterranean Sea. The tiered, colorful town I know and love appears far below me, and I am thrilled beyond expectations. Taking time to savor this moment so precious to me, I look around and appreciate the raw beauty in front of me. *How fortunate you are, Margie.* I want to remember this feeling for the rest of my life. I am all alone here, yet I do not feel lonely. The world is mine to embrace, and life is good. *Thank you, God, for allowing me to make this journey.* I don't think I can take too many photographs of what is presented before my eyes. My Nikon and iPhone cameras are working overtime.

The 7.8 kilometer walk from Bomerano to Nocelle is supposed to take three hours, but for me it ends up to be four, because I'm enjoying the experience without rushing through just to arrive at the endpoint. I would recommend everyone to take their time, breathe in the dramatic views, and reside in the moment with nature.

And yet another handmade devotional shrine to the Blessed Virgin captures my attention. Put together with small stones and a statue of Mary positioned on top of a large boulder, this outdoor holy spot becomes a place where I pause to say a prayer. In the natural surroundings high above the sparkling sea, I am so at peace.

Once I return to the path, I'm forced to traverse rocky, uphill areas where I literally must climb on my hands and knees to navigate the increasingly more challenging trail. The dirt path becomes quite steep now, and when I navigate downhill in these areas the difficulty intensifies. My feet keep twisting, causing me to slip multiple times. At least a dozen times I come close to losing my footing completely, and I start to pray, saying Hail Marys over and over.

I'm wearing decent shoes but not hiking boots, and perhaps they might have made a difference. I hate to admit it, but at one point I actually do take a fall and scrape up my arm in several places. I'm forced to sit down on the ground and look for some tissues to suppress the bleeding. As a nurse, I know it's nothing major, but I'm embarrassed as more hikers walk past me and stop to ask if I'm okay or if I need a doctor. After a ten-minute respite, I'm back on my feet, a little sore and bruised but ready to continue.

Momentarily I see a pair of black dogs playing with each other and a black cat farther down the trail. I think I must be nearing a town, and soon my curiosity is validated when I notice a church steeple, which means I am close to the town of Nocelle, where the trail ends. Continuing on, I spot some homes with laundry hanging from their balconies, and a railing made from sturdier tree limbs provides a secure feeling. A few hundred meters more down the footpath, I am invigorated when I reach a sign almost hidden in the greenery. It reads: "Communita Montana Costiera Amalfitana/ Nocelle (436 m) Rispetta la natura/ Numeri Utili/Note."

I understand enough Italian to read this sign, which states that Nocelle is 436 meters ahead, or roughly a quarter of a mile. The mountain community of the Amalfi Coast wants me to respect nature. Beneath this encouraging welcome is a more cautious message, warning visitors to be aware of the danger of falling rocks and to remember that the edge of the footpath is unprotected, with no wall or railing.

I think it's safe to assume that anyone walking here already knows this, but I guess the warning is warranted. I'm psyched to know that in a quarter of a mile I will be in Nocelle. Anticipating only another five or ten minutes of walking, I don't think I can be more elated. Along the way I see one of the mules I've heard so much about. Standing inside a stone barn behind an iron railing, he is able to stick his head out the half-door.

Once I arrive by myself in Nocelle, my feeling of achievement is beyond description. Tired, but ecstatic, I wander down a narrow stone pathway as I look for signs of the restaurant I've read about. I could use something cold to drink and a tasty meal. A wall comprised of rocks with greenery sprouting up between some of them abuts one side of this path, and along the other side is the beautiful sea. A white building with an open, white, wrought iron door interests me. Little do I know that I am at Villa Antica Macina, a B&B owned by an Italian woman named Amalia Durazzo (see Chapter 4).

***

The Amalfi Coast is tranquility and allure without limitations. This day is truly a highlight for me, and I'm ecstatic with my resolve to take on this adventure. This sense of accomplishment is so worth it!

Places I Have Yet to Explore

No amount of time in the world could ever allow me to visit every single locale on this rugged, majestic coast. Sure, I have my favorites, but stories I've heard and photos I've seen from other hilltop towns and coastal communities whet my appetite. I'm captivated enough to want to discover these places on future trips.

***

Cetara, one of the smallest seaside villages on the Amalfi Coast, has intrigued me for a long time, since this fishing village maintains its original character and is not on the radar of most tourists. I've been through this town a few times as a passenger on the SITA bus as it passes through, so I have an idea of its appearance. I recall seeing the typical laundry hanging on the lines and the residents dressed in casual attire as they go about their everyday lives. What I'd like is more time to truly experience Cetara.

With a population of only 2,141 and a geographic area smaller than five square kilometers, Cetara remains an authentic Italian coastal fishing village. This postcard-pretty town, its pastel-colored houses hugging the beach, enjoys the honor as one of Italy's nineteen most beautiful villages as listed by *The Telegraph* as recently as November of 2017.

Cetara's history dates back to the ninth century, when the Saracens established a settlement here. One of the recognizable sights here is Erchie, a sixteenth-century Norman watchtower, one of the best preserved on this coastline. Built atop a rock that overlooks the crystal blue waters of the Tyrrhenian Sea, Erchie is one of the few landmarks of Cetara. Another ancient tower, Torre di Cetara, graces the opposite end of the village and is a popular wedding venue and a museum today.

Cetara is synonymous with tuna and is renowned throughout the world, since massive quantities are exported to Japan for use in sushi dishes. The people here are called "i Cetari," taken from a name that meant tuna fish at one time. Today, tuna catches provide the *cetaresi* with their livelihood. Aside from the wooden fishing boats closer to shore, mammoth tuna trawlers sail out to deeper waters and travel as far as Sicily and back.

Nighttime *pescatori* (fishermen) leave in their boats equipped with powerful lamps as they fish for anchovies. Octopus and squid are a few of the common varieties of seafood that Cetaras's restaurants offer. Cetara is also famous for its *colatura di alici*, an amber-colored syrup prepared from anchovies fermented in brine for months.

Although I have not yet been here, I'd like to taste the fresh seafood offered at these three restaurants, all of which come highly rated: Ristorante San Pietro, for classic fare; Acquapazza, for contemporary cuisine; and Punto e Pasta, a casual restaurant rated #1 on Trip Advisor for food, ambience, price, and friendliness.

And, of course, I can't wait to photograph the beachfront with its colorful boats pulled up on the shore. I can also imagine what distinct photos I'll be able to capture of these hardworking fishermen in Campania.

***

For all the times I've been to Positano, I've yet to visit the tiny Laurito Beach, which is only a five-minute boat ride from Spiaggia Grande, the main beach of Positano. Perhaps next trip I'll get there. I understand this little-known beach derives its name from the abundant laurels that grow nearby. As tucked away as Laurito Beach is, half is private and the other half belongs to a hotel.

A free boat shuttle departs daily from Positano's main pier. I know I've seen the distinguishing red fish-shaped sign advertising Da Adolfo on the mast of this boat, but I never realized before now that it leaves every hour beginning at 10 a.m. for the five-minute ride to Laurito Beach. Not advertised in guidebooks, this beach used to be one of the best-kept secrets on the Amalfi Coast. However, it has become more well-known recently, and some of the locals suggest it has become a bit of a tourist trap. For this reason, reservations for the boat trip are necessary and can be made by calling the phone number on the Da Adolfo website. As of this writing, the number is (+39) 089875022.

I still plan to experience it myself, though. A wooden plank gangway off the boat directs passengers to the beach and to Da Adolfo Restaurant on the terrace above, where swimsuits are the accepted dress code. I'm told this easygoing restaurant on the beach boasts a history of more than forty years. The menu features pastas with all varieties of freshly caught seafood, grilled mozzarella on a lemon leaf, salads, antipasti, *dolci* (desserts) and, of course, vino. I'm hungry already. Like most seaside hotels and restaurants here, Da Adolfo is closed between October and April.

***

Atrani, an Amalfi Coast town situated just to the east of Amalfi, is considered the smallest community in southern Italy, with a surface area of only 0.12 square kilometers. Less than a thousand people call this their home, yet its seaside location makes it a perfect filming location for movies and, most recently, the initial scene of a fun Fiat commercial.

For me, one of the appealing features of Atrani is its soft, black sand beach, unusual for this coast which is most often identified with gray, pebbled beaches. Pastel-colored homes interspersed between white buildings on various levels define the landscape like an exquisite watercolor painting. On the ferry ride between Salerno and Amalfi, I can identify Atrani by the distinguishing architecture of the collegiate church of Santa Maria Maddalena. The prominent sixteenth-century bell tower and the yellow and green majolica tile domes can't be missed.

I'm reminded of a visit to a special exhibit of artist M. C. Escher's work, when one of his lithographs screamed *Amalfi Coast!* to me. As I later learned, the print was a view of Atrani from his perspective above the town. This 1931 work, titled "Atrani, Amalfi Coast," one of several in his *Metamorphoses* series, is not the only piece in which Santa Maria Maddalena appears. I understand Escher produced a beautiful crayon drawing of Atrani, in which he features a staircase. Another lithograph, titled "Dilapidated Houses in Atrani," is part of his collection as well. I'm tempted to purchase a copy of "Atrani, Amalfi Coast," but I have no more wall space in my home, after filling it with framed photographic images I shot during my travels and also some original art I've purchased in Italy over the years.

Pretty blue-and-white umbrellas cover the beach in the summertime. The highly recommended beachside restaurant, Le Arcate, with its wide terrace, welcomes guests in summer and winter to savor traditional seafood dishes for lunch or dinner. I envision Atrani as the place to soak up the sun in a relaxed atmosphere and experience *il dolce far niente*. Why haven't I discovered this gem of a place before now?

***

Situated between Praiano and Amalfi, in a valley near the sea, is the teeny commune of Conca dei Marini. This town of less than seven hundred people is a true fisherman's village, with nothing touristy about it except for its impressive Grotta dello Smeraldo (Emerald Grotto). These hidden caves, accessible only by rowboat, fascinate me. The magic of this grotto comes to life as the dark waters inside the thirty-meter-high cave are illuminated by sunlight. As the sun shines on the crystalline water inside the marine cavern, an emerald-green, shimmery hue reflects throughout the enclosed space. This magnificent sight is attributed to a phenomenon caused by sunlight filtering through an opening beneath the cave's surface. Sounds almost magical.

Discovered less than a hundred years ago by a local fisherman, this marine cave is a tourist attraction that I'd love to see. At a cost of only five euros, this experience seems like a bargain, and I am prioritizing it on my bucket list. On the floor of the cave, divers have installed a white ceramic nativity scene which, at Christmas time, becomes the focus of much interest.

I can't read anything about Conca dei Marini without learning about a special Campanian pastry that originated here. *Sfogliatella* Santa Rosa dates back to the seventeenth century, when one of the Dominican sisters from the Monastero Santa Rosa, a convent suspended high above the sea, created these shell-shaped, cream-filled, delectable *dolci*. Using dough leftover from making bread, the nun added sugar, milk, dried fruit, and semolina to make this luscious pastry which is forever connected to Conca dei Marini. These *sfogliatelle* are filled with sweet ricotta cream. What distinguishes the *Sfogliatella* Santa Rosa from all others is the dollop of cream and a black cherry on top. Several variations of the legend and the *sfogliatella* exist today, and in Naples, especially, the recipe is slightly different. The convent now is a five-star, luxury hotel, with its own Michelin-starred restaurant. Every summer the town pays homage to this sweet treat with a festival in August.

***

Furore is a town so small that its tiny beach nestled amid sheer rocky cliffs can only be glimpsed from a bridge thirty meters above the Gulf of Salerno. Although I've crossed this bridge as a passenger on more than one occasion, the driver of the vehicle in which I was riding made no effort to stop here, so I have yet to see this beautiful place. With less than eight hundred people and a land mass of 1.7 square kilometers, this village is not on most tourists' radar.

Most of Furore is not visible from the sea, and because it has no main piazza it is known as *paese che non c'è* (the town that doesn't exist). Instead, the village is comprised of a smattering of old fishermen's houses, painted in hues of muted pastels and constructed onto the ridges of the cliffs three hundred meters above the sea. The opening to the beach created by nature is a fjord, a gorge carved into the rock at the mouth of a deep valley that cascades down to the sea. This fjord's nickname is Fiordo.

I'd like to be here in the summer, when every year on the first Sunday in July, Furore hosts the world's best divers to compete in the Marmeeting High Diving World Cup. A platform is erected in the middle of the arched bridge along SS163 overlooking the fjord, and the participating divers leap off this diving platform twenty-eight meters above the Tyrrhenian Sea.

Another unique aspect of Furore is its artistic vibe. In 2006, the artistic event, Muri d'Autore (Walls in Search of Authors) launched as an initiative to present this overlooked village to more people. Since then, its success has grown and can be measured by what is happening today. Each September, artists from all over the world descend into Furore and paint images that depict the soul of this community on walls, houses, and any surfaces they can find, sharing their artistic talents with all of us. This open-air museum consists of over a hundred paintings, murals, and sculptures throughout the village, transforming Furore into a *paese dipinto* (painted village), and drawing more visitors, much to the delight of the town's administration. This would be reason alone to visit Furore, especially for anyone who loves art.

One more significant feature to this village is its claim to remarkably high-quality Costa d'Amalfi wine. Furore is one of only three communes on the Amalfi Coast that has permission to include its name on the label. At the highly recommended Le Cantine Marisa Cuomo, the wine growers tend to their vines completely by hand, and the cellars are built out of dolomitic-limestone rock. The vineyards produce red and white wines recognized by critics and respected all over the world. Tours and wine tastings can be arranged by contacting the winery and making a reservation. As of this writing, the email contact is reservation@marisacuomo.com, and the phone number is (+39) 333 4313667.

***

Praiano is one of the lesser-known jewels along Italy's famous Amalfi Coast. It's quiet, relaxed atmosphere makes this tiny seaside village of two thousand inhabitants a prestigious resort location. Built into the steep cliffs which overlook the sea and situated exactly halfway between Positano and Amalfi, ten kilometers from each city, Praiano offers stunning views. One can easily recognize the town by the cascade of white houses on the steeply sloping hillside.

Once just a sleepy ancient fishing village, Praiano is now a preferred tourist destination on the Amalfi Coast. Today the tiny, pebbled, Marina di Praia beach, protected on three sides by plunging cliffs, welcomes tourists. But this was once the place where fishermen would spend their time repairing nets, rebuilding boats, and cleaning fish. Today, old fishing boats, nets, and tools of the trade for those who make their living on the sea still cover the beach that looks like a travel poster. I understand Marina di Praia is reachable by walking down a coastal path beginning at Via Roma in Praiano and following along for about fifteen minutes. Not unexpected, some stairs are involved. By now I know that steps are always a probability anywhere on the Amalfi Coast, but the end result is so worth the challenge.

Famous for romantic sunsets and beautiful beaches, the westward facing Cala della Gavitella is the only beach on the Amalfi Coast promising sunshine all day until sunset. From here, I'm told, the view is nothing less than spectacular, with the Li Galli islands and distant island of Capri and the Faraglioni Rocks in sight.

My only experience of Praiano is from the corniche road high above the town. Its roadside *presepe* (Nativity scene), one of the most unique aspects of Praiano, is easily seen while traveling on the Amalfi Coast Road, SS163. Crafted by artist Michele Castellano, this *Praiano in miniatura* represents part of the existing rock wall. The fascinating display features tiny houses and models of some of the buildings in Praiano. Of course, the Nativity scene is prominent. Its location allows for a place to park a car to have a better look. Every Christmas season, the lighting of this Nativity grotto is a main component of Praiano's festivities, and I can only dream of experiencing such a beautiful sight during the holidays.

Not unlike the artistic project in Furore, Praiano also has developed its own art initiative, called NaturArte Project. With the intention of developing its own identity, a group of community leaders has encouraged artists to create ceramic plaques of art and stone sculptures to line the streets and pathways of Praiano along eight different routes. This unique street art contributes to the concept of an open-air museum in

101

Praiano, much in the same way as Ravello is identified with music. On my next trip to the Amalfi Coast, I'd like to find time to see these artistic creations.

***

The SITA bus winds through the center of Minori on such narrow streets that I can reach my hand outside the window and touch the lamppost on a wall. Other than riding through the town, I've not spent time in this quiet city next door to the larger town of Maiori. I recall meeting two travelers in Capri who told me they chose Minori because of its tranquil atmosphere and laid-back ambience. On the boat ride back from Capri, they pointed out their hotel with its marvelous, unobscured view of the shimmering sea. *Ah, this is the way to relax and soak in the peaceful waves of leisure.*

I could enjoy that serenity and the beach every day of my life, but I also understand that Minori is well-known for a particular pastry shop, Pasticceria Sal De Riso, located next to the sea on Via Roma. Reason number two to visit this little community. Although the bus drives right past this place, I've missed my opportunity and hope to make up for it next time I'm on the Amalfi Coast. My mouth is drooling right now as I envision the different choices of handmade *dolci* from here, like the lemon cake, ricotta and pear tart, and tiramisu. *Mmmmm.*

Minori also possesses a long-standing tradition of pasta-making, dating back to medieval times. Made in the mills powered by the river, these pastas would be hung outside to dry all over the town. A signature pasta is *ndunderi*, considered one of the oldest types of pasta in the world. *Ndunderi* is a type of gnocchi, prepared with flour, egg, ricotta, and Parmesan cheese, typically served with a simple *pomodoro* sauce and, of course, a few basil leaves. Minori's restaurant owners feature this pasta with a true sense of pride. The *Tagliolini al Limone* (lemon tagliatelle) is also one of Minori's most popular pasta dishes. *Note to self: Add these pasta specialties to my must-try list.*

***

On my next visit, I may heed the advice I've received from other travelers and check out Herculaneum or Paestum, neither of which I have visited. From what I'm told, the UNESCO World Heritage Site of Herculaneum is much smaller and not as grandiose, but far surpasses the more popular Pompeii in terms of the experience and the quality of the ruins. According to Dr. Andrew Wallace-Hadrill, British ancient historian, archaeologist, professor of Roman Studies, and Director of the Herculaneum Conservation Project at the University of Cambridge, Herculaneum is better preserved because the method of destruction differed from the Pompeii pumice. In Herculaneum, clouds of hot gas and ash, known as pyroclastic surges, blew through in waves, causing layers of this material to form into rock. In addition, the heat from the blast was much higher in Herculaneum, improving the town's preservation.

Due to the direction of the winds and its location west of Pompeii, Herculaneum was spared the initial onslaught of the erupting Vesuvius, so the slower-falling ash in the following days preserved the homes and everything else much better. Herculaneum was a richer city than Pompeii, so the preserved ruins of complete homes are more expansive, the mosaics are more impressive, and more of the marble still exists. A twenty-minute train ride from Naples, I'm tempted to explore Herculaneum next time.

Also a UNESCO World Heritage Site, and a thirty-minute train ride south of Salerno, is Paestum. Best known for its three well-preserved Greek temples that date back to 500 B.C., Paestum might be a better choice for an archeological excursion if staying in the southern end of the Amalfi Coast closer to Salerno. A Roman amphitheatre, partially aboveground, adds to the sites to see here. What makes Paestum different is that this city was never buried by Vesuvius, and unlike Pompeii and Herculaneum, the well-preserved ruins here are of Greek origin, rather than Roman. Lots of choices.

***

I'd like to add a few thoughts about Pompeii. While technically not on the Amalfi Coast, Pompeii is one of the most popular sights tourists visit during an Amalfi Coast vacation. Its reputation well-deserved, this UNESCO World Heritage Site attracts three million visitors each year and has been a tourist destination for more than 250 years. For these reasons, I'm including it here, not as a place I have yet to explore but as one I have visited — twice. I almost feel as if I haven't been to Pompeii though, because I'd have to rate both visits as less than enjoyable.

I remember my first visit in 2009 as interesting but more of a chore than a wonderful adventure, mainly because the entire two-hour guided tour occurred during pouring rain. Hector, the knowledgeable certified guide, tried his best and, to his credit, turned an unfortunate situation into an educational one.

My memories of the second time I traveled to the archeological site of Pompeii are from late September of 2013. Also a disappointing visit, this time due to extreme heat and crowds. I distinctly recall that after an hour and a half, my interest in seeing any more ruins had completely disappeared, in exchange for some ice water and a return to an air-conditioned hotel room. To be fair, my visits to Pompeii under less-than-pleasant circumstances cloud my opinion of these magnificent ancient ruins. I need to return on a good-weather day and anticipate being amazed.

***

Little-known secrets and hidden places abound on the Amalfi Coast, so every trip is always a new adventure. No journey is ever the same, and I welcome the excitement.

Delicious Experiences

One of the key ingredients in the Italian culture is food, and each of Italy's twenty regions highlights its own special cuisine. It's no secret that Italians pride themselves on the preparation of meals, using only the freshest ingredients. One of the rewards of traveling to Italy is the food. Thousands of restaurants exist in Italy, most of which are Italian. I almost laugh when someone asks for a recommendation of where to eat, since most establishments I stumble upon in Italy surpass my expectations. This is not to say that every single one is great, but I do recall some of my favorite food experiences on the Amalfi Coast—some fancy and some casual.

My preferred places are small, intimate restaurants where the owner acts as host, waiter, chef, or all three. During my three-month solo trip to Italy in 2011, I remember my inclination to want to eat earlier than the local Italians. The typical dinnertime in Italy is usually around 9:00 p.m., and most restaurants don't even open their doors until 7:30 p.m., at the earliest. On occasion, I would be the only person in the trattoria or *ristorante*, and these encounters are among my fondest in Italy.

From my travels, I've learned to engage in friendly conversation with the hotel's front desk manager and inquire about a restaurant recommendation, preferably a place where the locals like to eat. I'm never disappointed.

I remember doing this in 2014 when I stayed in Amalfi. The knowledgeable Italian man at the desk is happy to oblige and mentions several places, one of which is Da Maria Trattoria Pizzeria, a few steps away from the cathedral and a short walk from my hotel.

Since I'm in the mood for a pizza, an authentic, classical, Neapolitan-style pie in the Campania region of Italy sounds perfect to me right now, and I follow his directions to the restaurant on the busy Via Lorenzo d'Amalfi. The recommended trattoria is not crowded yet, since it's still early evening, but half of the outdoor tables are occupied by patrons, an indication that the food must be good.

A sign near the entrance lists a menu, and after a quick look, I walk inside and ask to be seated. Not a fancy place, Da Maria's décor fits perfectly with its name. Along a solid white wall, approximately twenty blue ceramic holy water fonts with different images of the Virgin Mary decorate the walls. The ambience is pleasant with an undeniable family feel. The wonderful aroma of pizza as it bakes fills the air. I think I'm home.

This family owned restaurant is a mainstay in the heart of Amalfi, with its owner, Luigi Pisacane, managing the kitchen of the restaurant he purchased in 1968. At that time, only five tables made up the trattoria that he named in honor of his wife, Maria, who encouraged him in this business endeavor. The food is freshly made from local seasonal ingredients, and a full wine cellar guarantees plenty of choices for his guests.

Next time I may have to try the *diavola* (devil pizza), which is topped with spicy salami and peperoncino.

***

Certain food experiences remain uppermost in my mind whenever I think back to my Italy travels. This one, simple as it may seem, makes me smile every time I remember the event. The year is 2007, and my brother Rick, my sister-in-law Monica, and I are staying in Sorrento at Hotel Central, a moderately priced hotel on Corso Italia in the heart of the city, and only seven hundred meters from the Circumvesuviana train station. I laugh out loud as I write this because I recall the day we arrived at that station. The walk to the hotel took thirty minutes, thanks to a wrong turn we made. I admit I am not that great with directions, and Monica tells me Rick isn't either. A three-night stay provides us with a comfortable place to call home as we explore Sorrento.

One of the best aspects of this hotel is its enchanting rooftop terrace with a panoramic view of the city and surrounding southern Italian countryside. In the afternoon, we find ourselves alone on the landscaped garden rooftop and sit down at an empty wrought iron table that appears so inviting. Wearing light jackets, we are warmed by the sun on this beautiful October day. A menu is provided for us, and after a quick once-over, we make our decision and order lunch. The unique feature here is the ability to call in the order using a hotel phone situated on the wall, and a server will deliver the meal when it is ready. We don't have to think too much, because on this trip, my first to Italy, I am content to eat pasta *pomodoro* at almost every meal, and so are Rick and Monica. So, rigatoni *pomodoro* and Diet Coke it is, for the three of us.

Not minding the wait for our food on this delightful outdoor patio, we begin to unwind. "I can't believe we are in this relaxing place. What a contrast to that train from Naples," Monica says.

"Oh my God," I say, "I just want to forget about it. This place is heaven."

"I can see the tracks over there, and a train is coming," Rick says. "The view from here is amazing. This rooftop is great."

Soon our waiter arrives, bringing platters of Italian pasta for the three of us. The rigatoni, lightly sprinkled with Parmesan cheese, looks exactly like my Grandma Savoca's. After Rick tastes the sauce, he validates the sentiment. "Not only does this look like Grandma Savoca's, but the taste is identical." I have to agree, having grown up with her rigatoni and meatballs my entire life. *Does life get any better than this?*

***

Another memorable food experience of mine is from a day in Sorrento, this time in 2013, when I am the lucky guest of Tina Carignani, expert tour guide and owner of Discover Napoli Destinations. She's driving, and once we arrive in Sorrento, she parks her car and escorts me to one of her favorite haunts, Pizzeria da Franco. A landmark in Sorrento for years, this casual, family run restaurant is like no other.

The wooden-bench picnic tables that fill the room create a rustic look, but what really draws my attention are the dozens of large prosciuttos—at least fifty—that hang from hooks attached to tracks along the ceiling.

"Franco's has a reputation for its pizza and panini," Tina explains, and she decides I need to try the latter. "Do you know what saltimbocca is?" Clueless, I shake my head. "Saltimbocca is a specialty of Sorrento. It's a panini made with pizza dough in a coal-fired oven." *I guess I won't be trying to replicate this when I return to the States.* "Like a sandwich, you have your choice of what goes inside."

"That sounds delicious. I think I'll have the one with fresh mozzarella and *pomodori*."

"Great choice," Tina says.

Once my saltimbocca arrives, I open it to see how it's made. The melted mozzarella clings to the warm, browned, thin pizza dough, and *pomodori*, basil, and a few diced pieces of black olive are mixed in. The sandwich is hot, and as I bite into it, I'm sold on saltimbocca.

"Oh my God! I love it. This is so good," I manage to say between bites.

"Of course you do. I knew you'd enjoy it." Tina is beaming, and when it's time to leave she refuses to let me pay for lunch.

She lingers behind, talking in Italian with the owner, Signor Franco, while I take note of the wall decorations. Paintings of scenes in Italy grace the bright red-and-yellow walls. I also notice the cookies and pasta for sale in the window. I wait outside for Tina, who meets me in a few minutes. She is holding a little cellophane bag. Imagine my surprise when she hands it to me as a gift.

"I thought you'd like these Italian almond cookies," she says with her magnetic smile. She already knows about my sweet tooth. How can I every thank her for such generosity?

"Okay, now I'm taking you to meet Signor Pollio. He owns the oldest *pasticceria* (pastry shop) in Sorrento." Say *pasticceria* to me, and I'm there. Bar Pollio, also known as Pasticceria Pollio, isn't far from Da Franco, less than a five-minute walk on Corso Italia. Behind the long counter filled with pastries of all sizes and shapes is a gray-haired, middle-aged man wearing a light colored polo shirt. "Buona sera, Signor Pollio," Tina says, greeting the owner as he walks out from his place behind the counter. They embrace like the longtime friends they are. I love how the Italians are so unrestrained in sharing their emotions. "Voglio che incontri la mia amica, Margherita, dall'America," she says to him, introducing me as her friend from the US.

I smile and greet the gentleman, turning my head to accept the traditional two Italian kisses, one on each cheek. "Buona sera, Signore. Piacere di conoscerla." He and Tina continue to talk while I check out the sugary delights. This is a wonderful shop filled with all kinds of pastries and *dolci*, but my eyes are on the biscotti. Just as Tina promised, the biscotti I had tasted in Rome are here. I have not been able to find these specific biscotti anywhere else until now. The name is *biscotti all'amarena napoletani* (biscotti with a black cherry filling). My eyes light up as I see an entire tray of these delectable treats. The rectangular cookies are made with a short crust pastry and filled with sponge cake, black cherries, cherry syrup, and cocoa, creating a delicious taste. Signor Pollio is happy to wrap up six large biscotti for me, and Tina purchases a bag of the smaller versions. I am thrilled as I anticipate snacking on these in the next few days. When it's time to go, Signor Pollio refuses to allow either of us to pay, giving us the biscotti as a gift.

***

A highlight of my stay in paradise is an elegant lunch at La Sponda, the Michelin star-rated restaurant at Le Sirenuse Hotel. This historic Positano hotel has been in the Sersale family since 1951, when Marchesi Sersale converted their summer villa into a beautiful hotel. In keeping with the look of a home, this 58-room luxury hotel sits high above the Bay of Positano, affording views to die for. Today, owner Antonio Sersale maintains the tradition and look of a well-appointed palazzo while creating the attention to detail that makes Le Sirenuse a member of the prestigious Leading Hotels of the World. The exclusive restaurant is booked every night, as guests dine in an elegant atmosphere lit by four hundred candles.

My travel companions and fellow bloggers, Victoria and Susan, are honored, as am I, to be their guests for lunch on this sunny day, and we arrive promptly for our 12:30 p.m. reservation. We are immediately welcomed with a warm smile by Giovanni Ciccone, the director of operations. He soon introduces us to Vincenzo Galani, the maître d', who ushers the three of us out to the covered terrace, where our sage-linen-covered table overlooks Positano and the sparkling blue Tyrrhenian Sea. The Li Galli islands stand in the distance, and the sailboats anchored near shore add to the magical scene below.

"Oh my God, this could easily be the setting for a movie," I say as I stare at the magnificent view. Susan and Victoria are in awe as well, and we stand gawking for a minute before taking our seats.

Inside, entwined green vines hug the white columns, and magenta bougainvillea climb up the walls, creating a lovely garden appearance. We take our seats at the table, and the warm breeze makes for a pleasant, comfortable setting for *pranzo* (lunch).

Our lunch begins with prosecco and a tasty appetizer made with asparagus cream, buffalo ricotta, and olive oil. Its smooth consistency adds to the savory flavor. A surprise touch is a plate of Tuscan olive oil served on Vietri hand-painted plates and a basket of local bread, white and whole wheat. *Delizioso!*

A local Costa d'Amalfi white wine is next, and Salvatore, our sommelier, serves us a Tramonti Bianco per Eva from Tenuta San Francesco winery in neighboring Tramonti. He explains that this wine is a blend made from three varieties of grapes — Falanghina, Pepella, and Ginestra. Since these small wineries rarely export to the States, I am pleased to taste this regional local wine which is considered one of the best in Campania.

We are then treated to an arugula salad as well as Insalata Caprese Sirenuse, a tomato and buffalo mozzarella salad served with balsamic vinegar. Saverio, our efficient and knowledgeable head waiter, informs us that the *aceto balsamico* is produced in Modena and has aged twenty-five years. Only the best.

The three of us are enjoying this five-star VIP treatment, and we're just getting started. I can hardly wait to see what comes next. Everything so far is more than I could have anticipated. Two tasty-looking appetizers soon appear. The first is *alici del golfo marinate, olio, sale e limoni della costiera* (white anchovies marinated in olive oil, salt, and lemons of the Amalfi Coast). The second is *carpaccio di pesce con insalata di finocchi, pinoli, e olive nere* (fish carpaccio seasoned with fennel, pine nuts, and black olives). Ordinarily I am not fond of anchovies, but I am surprised how much I enjoy the taste when they're prepared in this manner. *Tutto buono!*

When we're ready for the main entrée, I choose today's special, based on Saverio's recommendation—fresh ravioli pasta with pesto and *pomodoro*. When the dish arrives, I marvel at the plate, since I have never seen pasta presented in such a colorful and artistic manner. The creamy sauce of tomato, pesto, and cheese covers the ravioli in a pleasing, ribbonlike design in the colors of the flag of Italia. Not only is the presentation enticing, but the pasta is especially appetizing. "How beautiful," I exclaim. "This is almost too pretty to eat."

Victoria's dish arrives and appears equally tantalizing to the eye as well as the palate. She chooses a grilled seafood medley which includes octopus, prawns, and two other types of perfectly prepared fish in a light lemon sauce. Susan chooses *paccheri* pasta (traditional Neapolitan pasta which resembles a huge, short rigatoni) with a medley of seafood and small tomatoes mixed in a light wine sauce.

"My goodness!" Susan says. "Everything looks gorgeous."

This special team of sophisticated waiters attired in white shirts and black pants are so quick to attend to our every need, yet they maintain a low profile, and their efforts result in a VIP experience beyond any expectations. Victoria, Susan, and I are having the best time. The atmosphere is lovely, and I can't imagine a better way to spend an afternoon.

After the meal, Gianluca, a waiter in training, arrives to present us with Le Sirenuse's own brand of limoncello, followed by espresso and a plate of Italian cookies. As if this isn't enough, he serves us their specialty dessert, *torta caprese al cioccolato* (chocolate almond cake). The cake is to die for, and I simply can't resist it.

Every aspect of this afternoon is extraordinary, and I thank Le Sirenuse for the magnificent lunch at La Sponda and the unforgettable memories that will last until my next visit to Positano. Thank you from the bottom of my heart.

I would have liked to meet Antonio Sersale in person, but he isn't here today. I'm thrilled, though, to present my latest book, *Colors of Naples and the Amalfi Coast*, to Giovanni, who promises to give it to the owner. I hope to return one day and perhaps have the opportunity to thank him in person for a dining experience I'll never forget.

***

For the sweet taste of *dolci* in Positano, La Zagara is my favorite place to go. While sauntering down these alleys one morning in June of 2009 with my friend and travel companion Sue, I'm excited as we approach La Zagara. If the aroma drifting out of the front door doesn't lure me inside, the tempting pastries in the front window are too much to resist. "This is supposed to be the best in Positano for cannoli and other sweets. Shall we go inside?"

"Sure, I could use a cappuccino and something sweet," Sue says with a smile.

A hostess seats us at a table in the garden, and I can't wait to order a cannolo with a bit of chocolate around the edge and a cappuccino. Sue chooses a sweet lemon tart, which looks divine with the added touch of whipped cream. In existence since 1950, this *pasticceria* and restaurant does not disappoint.

Fast-forward to October of 2016, and I'm back in Positano at La Zagara. I decide to treat myself to lunch on the lovely outdoor terrace built among the trees and flowers, where the atmosphere transforms into a fragrant garden. Hand-painted ceramic tables ooze the colors of the Amalfi Coast. The experience is every bit as delightful as the first time, and my panini is delicious.

***

Since my plans on this solo trip are to stay in Positano for two weeks so I can finish my novel, I don't want to eat at a restaurant for every meal. After making a few inquiries from the locals, I discover a *negozio di alimentari* in the center of town. Vini and Panini, also known as The Wine Shop, becomes an almost daily stop for me. This wonderful store, which has been serving residents and tourists alike since 1890, doubles as a small grocery, wine shop, and deli.

The owner, as well as some of his employees, speaks Italian and English. Since Positano is such a tourist town, I'm not surprised. In many cities in Italy where tourism is a major part of their economy, English is spoken quite a bit. I remember the first time I went to Italy and attempted to ask a police officer in Sorrento for directions in Italian. He stopped me and said, "Do you speak English?" After I nodded, he proceeded to give me directions in perfect English. I still laugh about it every time I repeat the story.

Everyone here is friendly and will make practically anything one desires. The selection of fresh produce—both inside and outside of the shop—more than satisfies my needs.

After browsing for five minutes, I select a couple of handfuls of the reddest, ripest tomatoes on the vine, a bottle of extra virgin olive oil, some balsamic vinegar, and a bottle of prosecco. Then I ask the clerk behind the deli counter for some fresh buffalo mozzarella and some fresh basil. After weighing the mozzarella, she disappears and returns with a huge clump of basil that looks as if it was just picked from her garden. With a smile and special care in wrapping everything, Maria hands me my package. I marvel at the reasonable price, especially for the basil, which costs fifty euro cents. The entire bill is less than twenty-five euros. I can't wait to get back to my hotel room where I can prepare my own lunch and savor it on my private balcony as I enjoy the rhythmic waves of the sea. Life doesn't get much better than this on the Amalfi Coast.

Five Days in a Monastery in Maiori

Maiori is part of the beautiful Amalfi Coast and located just five kilometers past the town of Amalfi. The SITA bus ride from the train station in Salerno is a stunning drive along the coastal road and steep cliffs and probably the best €1.50 for my money since arriving in Italy almost eight weeks ago. Maiori has the longest beach of any of the towns along the Amalfi Coast, and the residential section of the town is located up in the cliffs.

The year is 2011, and I am staying at a Franciscan monastery where a few friars still reside. My accommodations are arranged via the booking company Monastery Stays, specializing in reservations at convents and monasteries throughout Italy and other countries. A substantial number of these facilities no longer need all the rooms for nuns and priests, so they are now used as guestrooms for travelers. In my experience, I find them to be spartan, but immaculate, and located in central parts of the cities. Most have a curfew, and the doors are locked after that time. I'm not a late-night person in Italy, so the time works well for me. I like booking a stay at a convent or monastery occasionally, especially in cities where hotels are expensive, so I can save some money.

Later I will learn that some of these accommodations are also able to be booked in other ways, allowing the traveler to save the fees charged by Monastery Stays. Some are listed as B&Bs, and others allow direct bookings through the property at an even lower cost. Most of the time the two-night requirement still holds. An interesting note is that some of these places are also dorm rooms connected to Catholic universities, such as one I reserved in Bologna, and in those places no curfew applies.

This fifteenth-century monastery sits right on the Amalfi Coast Road along the sea, and from my window I have an unobstructed view of the water. Although this monastery is not air-conditioned, the breeze off the sea makes my room quite comfortable, even at the end of May. A long promenade between the street and the shore distinguishes this city from others along the coast. On this boardwalk, people dressed in casual summer clothing amble past bars, *gelaterie*, and restaurants. Like the locals, I stroll up and down and familiarize myself with what I see here. The road that runs along the beach is slightly elevated, and opposite from the road are lots of inviting restaurants.

After attending an early evening Mass at the Church of St. Francis next to the monastery, I walk down the promenade to the interesting-looking Ristorante La Vela. I remember reading some recommendations about this restaurant and decide to try it for dinner. Welcoming me as if I am an old friend, the amiable male host directs me to a table with a view to die for. As a solo traveler, I'm surprised to receive such a special perk. Although I didn't order an appetizer, I am served some seaweed bruschetta prior to my dinner. "Complimenti dallo chef," the waiter says.

"Grazie mille," I reply. The strands of seaweed prepared on a lightly toasted slice of bread, drizzled with olive oil and garlic, create an appealing dish. Not so adventurous in trying new foods at this point in my Italy travels, I taste it and, to my surprise, I like it. A glass of wine, pasta *pomodoro*, and *insalata mista* complete my meal, as I savor the ambience of this beachfront restaurant and the taste of my favorite food. *Delizioso!*

After a good night's rest in my simple, yet spotless, single room in the monastery, I arrive in the breakfast room to find it nearly empty. I discover that I'm one of only two guests staying here. The priest and a woman who works here speak only Italian, as does the other guest, a woman from Rome. One advantage of this situation for me is the opportunity to practice speaking the language. They seem pleased that I understand them and can converse in Italian.

I have no agenda for the day, and it just so happens that the proprietor of the historic Castle of San Nicola is here this morning. The friendly woman employed at the monastery asks me to join her later this morning when she drives this gentleman up to the castle at eleven.

"Grazie, sono molto felice di andare," I say, thanking her and expressing my delight at the invitation.

Although my plans do not include a visit to this castle, I now ask myself, *why not?* Then I can walk back for some exercise. My brother Rick will enjoy hearing about this, although I know for a fact that he would have declined the ride, opting to walk there and back.

After my simple breakfast I wander outside. The sun is shining and the air feels warm. I cannot believe I am staying along the Amalfi Coast, with a view of the sea and the sounds of the ocean waves at night. This alone would be an ideal vacation. Everyone here is very friendly, greeting each other with a *buongiorno* or *buona sera*. A lot of the little shops look appealing, and I will definitely have to check them out later. One is a sandal shop, where I catch a glimpse of the owner and his wife sewing the sandals inside their store.

As I sit in a beautiful courtyard at the monastery with a pergola shading me from above, I can smell the pleasant citrus aromas from the enormous lemons that are growing on the trees just above the pergola. Hanging handmade ceramic lights adorn this peaceful setting where birds warble. Not unexpected, I notice a shrine to St. Francis in this quiet space. I understand that Roberto Rossellini, the famous Italian director, chose this garden as a filming location for scenes in his 1946 award-winning film, *Paisà*.

The terrace, a very tranquil spot, becomes a wonderful place for me to write, and I'm glad I planned to spend five days here. Since it's too expensive for me to stay at a hotel with a sea view in Maiori, I'm thrilled to find this monastery with its affordable rate of eighty euros a day, a true bargain for this sought-after location in Italy.

At eleven o'clock I am ready to take the ride to the castle, but apparently I misunderstood the invitation from yesterday. The woman is not going; instead, I learn that it is just me and Crescenzo, the seventy-three-year-old proprietor. Dressed in loose blue jeans and a blue-and-white plaid shirt, he walks me out to his car in the parking lot. We communicate in Italian, and so far, so good. I'm game and figure this will be a new experience. So I get into Cresenzo's car and off we go. Of course, I realize too late, once Crescenzo drives the vehicle as far as the road goes up the mountain, he parks, and we now have to climb over three hundred steps to the abandoned castle. I'm not so sure my feet agree with my earlier consent. (Rick will undoubtedly smile when he reads this!) After Cinque Terre, though, this isn't too bad, and I remind myself that Crescenzo climbs these steps every day. I must admit that he can move a lot faster up the steps than I can, and he doesn't even need to stop to take any breaks. I'm embarrassed that he is in better shape than I am.

Once we arrive at the castle, it seems that I have my own personalized tour with Crescenzo as guide, since nobody else is waiting. The situation turns out to be a blessing in disguise, and I'm glad for the chance to explore a place most tourists never even know exists. The castle is principally ruins at this point but still makes for an exciting excursion.

Crescenzo takes care of repairing things at the castle, as well as tending to his lemon trees and grapevines. His eagerness to show me everything here proves how much this man loves doing this work. The view from the top of the mountain is magnificent, not only of the town of Maiori, but points farther away. Crescenzo draws attention to the town of Ravello, with its famous landmarks, Villa Rufolo and Villa Cimbrone, on the next mountain high above Amalfi. For me to see these historic places from this vantage point warms my heart, and the perspective is so different from my earlier visit to Ravello.

After the tour finishes, I offer Crescenzo twenty euros, although not once does he ask for a fee. A donation jar sits almost unnoticed, and for a personalized tour like this the amount is more than worth it. Thanking me, Crescenzo shows his appreciation. I leave there with a freshly picked lemon and another memory of a kiss from an Italian man over the age of seventy. I think I am becoming accustomed to this Italian habit. He is just a kind gentleman with a genuine smile that I'll never forget. "Ciao, Crescenzo. Grazie mille."

I wave goodbye and start the walk down the hill on a real road, as opposed to the staircase we took coming here. I admit the downhill trek is much easier than the ascent. On the way back to town, I stop at a mini-market and buy some local provolone, salami, and fresh *pane* (bread). Then I return to the monastery and walk upstairs to my room to change clothes and grab a towel for the beach, pondering how lucky I am to have a place to stay so near the sea.

On the pebbly beach, I choose a spot close to the water and settle in to savor my homemade panini. The warmth of the sun against my skin eases the aches from my challenging hike this morning. Sitting here on the beach doing absolutely nothing relaxes me, as the sounds of the waves almost lull me to sleep. A few meters away I hear joyful laughter and song from some teenage boys having fun together. After some time, I walk into the sea, my sandals still on since the stones make walking barefoot too painful. I find the water temperature refreshing, and I think the weather in late spring is more pleasurable than in October. I am thoroughly relishing this day that began with no agenda.

***

The drive along Italy's Amalfi Coast is one of the most beautiful anywhere, especially as a passenger. For a few euros I can take a SITA bus from one town to the other and take in the incredible scenery along the Amalfi Coast Road from Maiori to Minori, Amalfi, Positano, and other villages in between.

I hope these bus drivers are compensated well, because navigating a commercial bus on these steep winding roads, as well as the narrow streets within the towns, is a feat nothing short of a miracle. I'm sitting in the seat directly behind the driver, and I watch with concern as another large bus approaches on a curve, and there is no room for both. These drivers must be familiar with the situation enough to observe a protocol I'm about to witness. The bus coming uphill must back down the road to allow room for the bus traveling downhill. Both vehicles literally pass within inches of each other, and if I tried, I could reach outside the window and touch the other bus. An awesome, if not scary, experience.

***

During my time here in the south of Italy, I have noticed some interesting things. There is a definite difference in the way people dress, in comparison to northern Italy. Now that the temperatures are in the eighties every day, I notice a lot of young Italian men dressed in shorts. Perhaps it is partly due to the climate, but I see far fewer women wearing scarves and stiletto heels here. I also must amend my previous impressions about the Italian bus drivers, as I now observe that some are more than helpful. Another practice that appears prevalent here relates to dogs, who seem to be welcome everywhere in Italy. I spot them on buses, trains, boats, in stores, restaurants, and on tours. One bar even has a bowl of water and a specific section marked "Dog Bar."

Having this kind of time in Italy to contemplate the Italian way of life allows me to make observations, some of which create more of an impact upon me than others. Each region in Italy is known for certain items, either grown or produced in that area, such as olive oil, wine, ceramics, and lemons. The Italian people who live in each area are proud of the items coming from their region; they are eager to share anything they can. It may be as simple as taking a lemon from their tree, scraping a little of its skin, and allowing me to smell its strong flavor.

I also realize how much the people identify with the earth and appreciate whatever grows there naturally, using various herbs and plants to their benefit. Rather than taking these things for granted, the Italians have such a passion and appreciation for what grows around them; they tend to the soil to reap the most use from it.

***

On the last day in May, after a return from Capri, I walk down to the end of the promenade and find the ceramics shop I have read about during my research for this trip. I'm thrilled the shop is open when I arrive. Ceramica L'Arte Vietrese greets me with its colorful storefront, and its partially open door beckons me to step inside. A huge selection of hand-painted vases, plates, mugs, tabletops, statues, pots, and more fills the floors and walls of this family-run shop. All the ceramics are made by hand by skilled artisans in Vietri, ten kilometers from here, and the prices as well as the products and selection are excellent.

Pasquale, the owner, greets me with a gracious smile and inviting voice. "Welcome! Please come in and look around. Perhaps you'll see something you like." He's a big man with jet-black hair and brown eyes, and I spend a lot of time conversing with him in English, since he demonstrates such excellent English language skills. During our conversation, he takes time to translate for his petite, pretty wife, Maria. He introduces her, and I speak Italian as much as I can so she is included in the conversation. I take an instant liking to this couple. Not only do they treat me well as a customer, but as a human being. Both of them are so personable, and from the respectful way Pasquale speaks of and treats his wife, he reveals that he has great honor and love for her. Engaging with them and enjoying the interaction tempts me to want to stay here and just hang out. I buy a few inexpensive ceramic items I need for gifts, and then I cannot resist buying one more piece for myself.

A family-operated business like this illuminates an appealing aspect of the culture of the Amalfi Coast and its people. The combined qualities of beauty and initiative inspire me and renew my love for this southern stretch of Italian coastline. I will definitely return here before I leave Maiori, at least to say goodbye to Pasquale and his lovely wife.

On the way back to my room at the monastery, I buy a slice of pizza at one of the restaurants along the *lungomare* (seafront). As I walk, I savor every bite and smile as I feel the soft breeze caressing my face. I listen to the whisper of the gentle waves as they roll in from the sea and think how fortunate I am. Lots of families with young children stroll and converse in the typical animated fashion, evidence of them enjoying the simple lifestyle. I can't be any happier than I am at this moment. If I had a way to bottle this feeling and take it home with me, I would.

While walking back I stop in at the sandal shop I noticed my first day here. I'm captivated as I watch this sandal maker work at his table in his tiny shop, as he creates a pair of leather sandals by hand. He looks up and acknowledges me with a smile. When I ask his permission to observe, he responds with a slight dip of his head. "Prego," he says. It's a word used often in Italy, one with a variety of meanings. In this case, it means "of course."

These shops are often a two-person operation, consisting of the owner and his wife, neither of whom are high-powered salespeople. They exude a sense of pride in what they do, confident in knowing that they design and construct a quality product. In my experience here and at other shops similar to this in Capri and Positano, the owners are happy to answer my questions and share information about themselves and their business.

They radiate happiness and certainly know how to make me feel welcome, even though my Italian is not the best. The prices are surprisingly reasonable, and I love the white, backless sandals with flowers I purchase from him. They are not only attractive, but comfortable as well. The twenty euros I pay for them is a bargain, and they'll also make a great souvenir from my travels.

Sandali Tipici Calzature Artigianali is located at 38 Lungo Mare Amendola in the heart of Maiori. Alfonso Dattilo, a leather master's son, began the sandal company over forty years ago, and Gerardo, third generation, continues the tradition today with the same fervor and dedication.

Now that I'm back at Casa di San Francesco, my home away from home, I settle in at a table on the veranda. This outdoor terrace a few hundred yards from the Tyrrhenian Sea creates a serene place to meditate and write. The fragrant citrus air is my little slice of heaven on Earth today. Completely surrounded by fresh lemons still on their branches, I feel a peaceful repose. I close my eyes and dream, and when I awaken, I'm inspired to put pen to paper.

***

This morning as I peer out my window, thick gray clouds fill the sky, a stark contrast to yesterday's sunshine. I'm guessing the forecast calls for rain. *Thank you, God.* I am so grateful that yesterday's excursion to Capri is now a treasured memory, rather than a soggy one. Today is a good day to stay inside and write and possibly catch up on doing some laundry by hand in the sink in my bathroom.

This monastery provides no Wi-Fi access, but I remember a sign advertising Wi-Fi in one of the nearby hotels. With umbrella in hand and my writing materials in my bag, I head outside. The rain starts before I can finish the two-minute walk up the street to Hotel San Francesco. Not sure whether I'll be allowed to sit in their sumptuous lobby and use the Wi-Fi, I approach the front desk manager and propose the idea to utilize their internet connection for a reasonable fee. To my delight, he agrees, and tells me the price will be ten euros for three hours—a great deal, in my estimation.

The spacious, well-appointed lobby, decorated with lush palm trees in beautiful containers carefully arranged on the terra-cotta-hued, ceramic tile floors, provides an attractive place for me to call my writing office today. Numerous comfortable white loveseats arranged in an attractive design complement the expansive, white, arched ceiling and glass chandeliers. As much as I enjoy my simple accommodations with a view at the monastery, I'm thrilled to embrace this lavish lifestyle today. I appreciate this opportunity to catch up on my blog writing in the comfortable and plush atmosphere of this four-star hotel on this rainy day in Maiori. My timing cannot be any better, as the rain increases in strength and persists for the next three hours.

As I glance around, I notice several people I recognize from the boat to Capri yesterday, and we strike up a conversation and compare some of our impressions. They speak English, and I'm happy to meet people who are as excited as I am about traveling in Italy. One aspect of traveling solo can be loneliness. Since I'm friendly and enjoy meeting people, shyness doesn't enter the equation on my travels.

My three hours is almost up, and the rain slows to just a drizzle, so I decide to leave this hotel and walk in the direction opposite the monastery, back toward the ceramics shop. In case I don't have a chance to visit tomorrow, I want to be sure to say goodbye to my friends there. When I arrive, I'm disappointed to find Maria isn't there, but Pasquale informs me that she will return soon. Within a short time, she enters through the front door with a smile on her face. I'm pleased, since I don't want to go home without a photo of Maria, Pasquale, and myself. Such unpretentious and caring people, they make me feel like I'm part of their family, and I'm so glad to have met them. I say my goodbyes but only after Pasquale presents me with a special gift for good luck. He hands me a small, flat, smooth, coral-colored shell and explains that it is the *occhio di Santa Lucia* (eye of Saint Lucy).

"Questo guscio viene da un animale del mare," he says, explaining that the shell comes from an animal of the sea, and it can only be given as a gift. I am flattered and moved to tears.

On my walk home, I return to La Vela for dinner and indulge with a glass of wine and marinara pizza. Once again, with compliments of the restaurant, I am treated to something special—a *bibita*, a refreshing drink made with orange, sugar, carbonated water, and lemon. And once again, the seaweed bruschetta appears at my table. I'm sorry to admit that I cannot eat all this tasty food.

Back in my room, I decide to go to sleep early, thanks in part to the wine. Tomorrow is a holiday when Italians celebrate the 150th anniversary of their country's unification. I wonder how the town of Maiori commemorates the event. All I know for certain is that the shops are closed all day.

***

At breakfast this morning, I'm told the weather forecast promises sunshine and warm temperatures. For me, that means a day at the beach. But first I walk to the nearby mini-market, where the shop owner is only too happy to make me a panini with the greatest of care and pride. I notice that the weights are listed in grams, so I try to calculate how much one hundred grams is in ounces while I wait. I think I recall that it's equivalent to about a quarter pound. As I'm watching him getting ready to pile that amount of salami on the bread, I have to ask him to go a little easy on the meat. "Per favore, Signore, piccolo salami. Grazie," I say. A shelf of fresh fruit attracts my attention while I wait, so I select a juicy, red, ripe plum. After paying for my purchase, I bid him arriverderci and walk down the street toward the beach.

What I like about the little shops in these towns is that most are run by their owners. The difference is noticeable, as they take particular pride in what they are doing. These owners make sure the entry to their shops is swept. They greet me, and they smile as they prepare my order. Even the wrapping is not simple, as they carefully package my purchase and tape it closed, sometimes even placing it into an additional bag. It's the little touches that make such a difference in their service.

Because of the national holiday, more local people than usual are on the beach, and I love watching them. A group of four young men, who appear to be about eighteen years old, are singing. Not something typically seen or heard on beaches in Florida, that's for sure. Italians love to sing, and although I was too young to remember, my older cousin John reminds me that my grandfather used to sing all the time. I wish I could recall those events, but he died when I was only nine. I do have fond memories of him, though, sitting outside under his apple tree and cutting up watermelon for my brothers and me to eat on hot summer afternoons.

The water here on the Amalfi Coast feels so refreshing, and even though these beaches are more rocky than sandy, I still enjoy them. I can see that these hardy local Italians are so used to the pebbled sand that they walk barefoot. Tourists like me do not.

I do love the scene of a beach surrounded by mountains of sheer rock that plunge down into the ocean. The sight is awesome, like a postcard, as Pasquale from the ceramics shop so accurately describes it. There really is no place quite like the Amalfi Coast, and this is truly a place where I could return year after year and never tire of it. Since my time here is nearing an end, and I must leave tomorrow, I make the most of my last day in Maiori.

***

This morning I must break away from this beautiful place. In contrast to the relaxation of yesterday, the day ahead will ultimately prove to be a day in which a number of things go wrong. It starts out badly and will continue on a downhill roll. I guess after eight weeks in Italy, not every day is going to be perfect.

At breakfast, an older Italian man approaches me while I'm eating alone at a table for two. He strikes up a conversation, and you guessed it, this is yet another man, about seventy-five years old, who seems to be attracted to me. I continue eating, not wanting to encourage him, but make small talk, hoping not to appear rude either. He continues to stand next to my table and talk to me in English with an Italian accent. He is persistent, giving no indication that he is going away. I wish he'd leave me alone, but instead, he stands there and offers to take me to Positano, Amalfi, and other places. He even admits that he is married, and his wife is not here with him. *What is the story with this guy?*

When I politely tell him I am leaving, he indicates that he wants to help me pack. I get up from the table, and despite shaking my head and bidding him arrivederci, he literally follows me to my room upstairs. When I tell him he cannot come with me, he pays no attention and continues talking and moving closer to me. I reach the door to my room, and no one else is around, so I'm a little nervous. But no way in hell is this man getting into my room. His refusal to take no for an answer and his aggressive behavior force me to physically stop him. I have to push him away with as much energy as I can muster before he finally turns around and departs. And we're in a monastery, a sacred place, too. *Thank God he isn't a big man. What is it with some of these old Italian men?*

As much as I enjoy being on the Amalfi Coast, I think I'm willing to say goodbye to Maiori for a while. Inside the safety of my room, I can't finish packing fast enough so I can leave and catch the bus to Salerno as soon as possible.

The checkout process isn't as easy as I hope today, as one more snag occurs for me. *God, please grant me patience.* I find out that I cannot pay by credit card, although the information on my reservation states otherwise. Since I don't have enough cash to pay for five nights here, I now have to look for a *bancomat* and withdraw money to pay my bill in cash prior to leaving. While I didn't anticipate an extra step, this is not such a big problem, because I know where the bank is, and I have time before I have to board the bus to Salerno.

After settling up my invoice and saying goodbye, I walk the short distance to the bus stop and wait in the scorching sun. In keeping with the rest of the morning, the bus is twenty minutes late, so I'm standing outside for forty minutes total. When my SITA bus arrives, it is packed with people who already boarded in Amalfi. What a sight I must be as I attempt to maneuver the steps alone with a suitcase. This perceived delay for the other passengers immediately causes comments from one irate Italian woman. At this point, I run short on patience and have no plans to keep quiet. I board the bus with my luggage and explain to her that I must get to the train station.

"Devo andare alla stazione ferroviaria," I say, nodding toward my luggage.

She shakes her head in disgust and keeps rattling in Italian. Luckily, several passengers disembark a few stops later, and I find a vacant seat and a place for my luggage. On days like this, I do miss my own car more and more. Life in Italy isn't perfect, and I know I have to take the good with the bad. Arriverderci, my Amalfi Coast.

Amalfi Coast Shopping Fun

One of the experiences I enjoy the most in Italy is shopping, and even if I don't plan to spend much money, I always come home with something that is an authentic item, usually handmade in Italy.

Sorrento is a place where shopping can entertain me for the entire day. I can get lost in the tiny alleys that branch off from Via San Cesareo, the narrow passageway and main shopping street in Sorrento. Filled with artisan shops and outdoor kiosks, this narrow shopper's haven teems with life all day and evening, except for a few hours in the afternoon when much of Italy pretty much shuts down. Handmade local products such as limoncello, leather crafts, ceramics, silk scarves, and more entice me as I enjoy the time browsing alone with no deadline.

One treasure I hope to find is a wooden music box crafted by hand using a special technique known as intarsia. This unique artistry is a method of creating an intricate design with a mosaic of wooden pieces and is a true art form that requires exceptional skill. Much to my delight, I encounter a shop that sells these inlaid wood boxes, and since the price is right at twenty-five euros, I purchase three of them. I'm not sure if I'll be lucky enough to find these anywhere else today, so for a deal as wonderful as this, I walk away happy.

Ten minutes later, I'm fortunate to discover what I'd really been searching for—an authentic inlaid wood shop owned by the craftsman himself. The darling Italian couple inside wins my heart in no time at all with their warm smiles and congenial welcome. He wears a loose, cranberry sweater over a red-and-white striped collared shirt, and she complements him with her light fuchsia-colored sweater over a black blouse. This attractive, color-coordinated, elderly couple definitely knows about fashion.

"Buongiorno, Signore e Signora. May I come in, please?" No other customers are inside their tiny shop, and they invite me to look around. More of a workshop than a storefront, long piles of wood in different colors cover the floor, and completed designs adorn every inch of wall space. Mixed in are some religious photos and a few green plants that look as if they could use some fresh water. I'm astounded by the choice of music boxes and jewelry boxes, not to mention the wall plaques and other items made with the intarsia process.

"Si. Where are you from?" the gentleman asks in perfect English.

My Italian is almost nil, since this is my first trip to Italy, so I'm grateful they speak English so well. "I'm American. My name is Margie, and my grandparents came from Italy. What is your name?"

The man answers, "I am Gaetano, and this is my beautiful wife, Rosa."

How sweet. My heart melts. "I'm happy to meet you both. Your shop is amazing. Did you make all of this?" I ask, incredulous at the talent before me.

"Yes, all of this," he answers.

Rosa beams with pride as she shares that her husband has been making inlaid wood products for sixty years. What I find even more remarkable is what she adds next. "Gaetano's family does this for two hundred years." The mere idea of a tradition handed down for that long within a family and involving at least four generations impacts me, and I am in awe.

I regret not discovering this shop first, but now that I'm here, I know I'm taking something back home with me. I peruse the selection of beautifully crafted boxes on my own for quite some time. On one of the shelves, two particular items capture my attention. Identical, small jewelry boxes with a pink inlay of a ballerina on top strike me as the perfect gifts for my three-year-old twin granddaughters. Katie and Emily take dance lessons at home in Florida, and these are souvenirs I hope they will cherish for a long time. When they get older, I will relay the story of Gaetano and Rosa and maybe even bring them here to Sorrento one day in the future.

Gaetano's watchful eyes and years of experience with people trigger him to make a subtle sales pitch, although not much of one is needed, as I've already decided to purchase the jewelry boxes.

"I make these with wood from olive trees in this area, in the countryside around Sorrento," he informs me. Then he points to the stacks of olive wood, waves me over to them to have a closer look, and points out the striations and wavy grain on the wood. For the acceptable price of thirty euros each, these one-of-a-kind, handmade intarsia boxes are a true value. The only thing missing from this lovely shopping experience is the chance to watch Gaetano creating his precious wood pieces while I am here. Perhaps I'll get the opportunity next time.

***

Italy is well-known as a fashion capital and *la bella figura* is always flaunted in some form or another. I enjoy window-shopping in Milan and Florence, despite the sticker shock of the apparel on display.

Based on my observations, southern Italy is more casual than northern Italy, with fewer rules and not as many examples of high fashion, especially in towns by the beach. On my first trip to Positano, I recall seeing the light, airy women's fashions displayed in the town's shops and windows, typical clothing for seaside resorts. Somewhat pricey for me, my experience has been limited to looking rather than buying, until now. It's June 2015, and for the first time, I'm staying in Positano for five days and nights. With much more time to explore the fashions here, I notice the trends of what is known as *Moda Positano*, or the Positano style. Hip, chic, colorful, light, and comfortable are words to describe this fashion style, and it's not something new. Back in the sixties, a Positano-born fashion designer named Giacomo Cinque, took over his family's business, a women's clothing shop named Antica Sartoria. Located directly on the beach, Antica Sartoria is easy to find for all the tourists who arrive by boat every day. The location as well as the product prove to be a recipe for success.

This store features fashions that are affordable as well as chic and luxurious and presents the Positano style. Embellished lace tops, tunics, denim jackets, ruffled skirts, ponchos, embroidered caftans, flared pants, beach bags, purses, and hats fill the shop from floor to ceiling. Today, three shops exist in Positano, two in Amalfi, two in Capri, and one in Sorrento, and others are located all over Italy, from Sicily to Venice. Prices range from high to low, and bargains are displayed on outdoor racks with signs advertising clothing marked down as low as five euros. Big-name celebrities return here year after year to shop for the fashions created by the well-known designer.

Let's see if I can find something I like at a good price, I muse. A helpful and friendly saleswoman allows me to try on my selections in a private dressing room and then offers suggestions and compliments as I step outside the fitting room to ask her what she thinks. I come away with three light, beach-type fashions, one that can double as a nightgown. The sleeveless, V-neck, white cotton fabric with a turquoise-blue marine design projects seaside to me, and the extra bling of tiny, turquoise-colored stones that look like sea pebbles sell me on this fun item that costs less than twenty euros. On the way out of the shop, I'm attracted to a flowing, smock-type, long-sleeved dress, one-size-fits-all, that will be great to sleep in. For less than ten euros, I buy it and leave with a smile.

Before I leave Positano, I return once more to one of their other shops and pick up a white blouse, one hundred percent cotton with embroidered beach designs in bright colors of coral and lime green. I love this new shopping find on the Amalfi Coast.

When Giacomo Cinque decided to produce his own line of clothing, he moved the production from Positano to India and expanded the business globally. With designer Riccardo Ruggiti, together they operate Antica Sartoria of Positano, which today also sells its products in stores far from Positano.

The turquoise tag inside the clothing reads, "Antica Sartoria by Giacomo Cinque," and the fabric care tag bears the words "Idea conceived from the house of Antica Sartoria of Positano and garment hand crafted by skilled Indian artisans. Produced in India conceptualized in Italy." So, although these fashions are no longer made in Italy, the concept originated here and the design is Italian.

***

When shopping in Italy, I prefer to purchase something particular to the region or town. For the Amalfi Coast, the main items include handcrafted ceramics, sandals, limoncello, and paintings by local artists. In almost every town I can find a limoncello shop by following my nose, because within one hundred feet of the store, the scent of fresh lemons permeates the area. The addicting aroma lures me inside the shop through no control of my own. Various sizes of bottles containing the special liqueur from the Amalfi Coast fill shelves outside the shop, but inside, an array of lemon-flavored or lemon-scented items are available for purchase.

I first spot one of these shops in Sorrento in 2007. Its name is Limonoro, a family-run business that dates back twenty years. The owners call themselves "Nino and Friends" and not only have stores in Sorrento and Capri, but far from the Amalfi Coast as well. While the production facilities are in Sorrento, other stores exist today in Siena and Venice.

Besides the limoncello, with its thirty-five percent alcohol content, other delights whet my appetite as I peruse the shop. My mouth waters as I see all the candies, like lemon and chocolate candied peel, and almond and lemon dragees, which have an almond center covered with subtle lemon-flavored chocolate. *Mmmm.* And there's more: limoncello drops, lemon marmalade, lemon cookies, panettone with lemon cream, and the regional babàs dipped into limoncello rather than the traditional rum.

In Positano, the lemon products shop is Sapori e Profumi di Positano, located in Piazza dei Mulini, and the scent is unmistakable and alluring. Inside the large shop are a plethora of items either made from or inspired by Sorrento lemons: handmade scented candles with the essence of lemons, lemon-infused massage oil, lemon soaps shaped like lemons, lemon perfumes, lemon candies and, of course, limoncello. Ceramic plates with lemon designs and fabric items with lemon motifs provide an amazing selection of Amalfi Coast souvenirs. Just walking past and enjoying the smell is sometimes all I need.

***

A product synonymous with the town of Amalfi is paper. Dating back to the twelfth century, the Amalfi people operated paper mills after learning the process from the Arabs. Today, a few mills still exist, and the handmade paper products are available at shops like La Scuderia del Duca. I have no problem locating this shop not far from the ancient Arsenali della Repubblica Marinara, or Arsenals of the Republic. I have always loved stationery. My drawers at home are filled with pretty notecards and writing paper, and I still enjoy sending a thank you in a handwritten note. So, I'm attracted to this store and enter the shop, glad I have time this trip to browse to my heart's content. The year is 2014, and I'm staying here for four nights.

Since 1980, Andrea De Luca and Giovanna Fusco have operated this shop, and plenty of tourists mill around inside as they check out the selection of merchandise. I'm not sure whether this man who works here is Signor De Luca, but he greets me with a smile and invites me to look around. I'm in my element as the clean aroma of books and papers envelops me. This shop features a variety of items, not all paper-related. Antique products, paintings, leather books, and calligraphy items are some of what is on display. But what attract me are the notecards and packets of writing paper with assorted designs that remind me of the Renaissance. Wedding invitations seem to be a big item here, as do cotton papers suitable for artists' use. I smile when I notice the sealing wax in twenty-two colors. Although it's an old-fashioned practice, the idea of using a brass sealing stamp with a wooden handle and wax to close an envelope in a personal way appeals to me. I guess part of me likes these outmoded ways, or maybe I'm just a romantic. I like that thought better.

Some of my friends also like to write notes, so the notecards will make perfect Christmas gifts for them later in the year. And since they don't take up much luggage space, always something I must consider when traveling to Italy, I decide to buy several sets of stationery and notecards, enough so I can keep some for myself. The prices are reasonable — between six and ten euros — so this is both a bargain and a meaningful memento from Amalfi.

***

Food may not be considered a shopping experience, but I'm including it as one here, especially since specific categories of food are available for purchase in their own shops. Gelato is one of those, and although I can also buy a gelato at a restaurant as a dessert, or sometimes in a bar, I prefer shops where authentic gelato artisans make the sweet treat on the premises every day.

I can still recall taking an evening stroll in Sorrento during my first trip in 2007, and stopping at a delightful gelato shop after dinner. I wish I could remember its name, but what I do recall is the delicious taste of the Sicilian cannoli gelato flavor. No one else is here except a friendly young woman behind the counter, and after she serves me, Rick, and Monica, we engage in a short conversation, since she speaks such good English. She shares that she is nineteen and that her father owns the shop, as well as the lemon grove across the street. However, her plans are to get an education and not work as a gelato server for the rest of her life. I'm inspired by her ambitions.

***

In Capri one of the top shopping experiences is a visit to Carthusia I profumi di Capri—or simply, Carthusia. Located close to the Giardini di Augusto, this perfume factory on Capri is one of the smallest in the world and began as a family business in 1948. The intent was to recreate the scent first made by the Carthusian monks in 1380 at the Certosa di San Giacomo, a monastery and one of the oldest structures on Capri. Today, Carthusia makes over a dozen different fragrances, employing the same production methods as the monks, so the tradition remains alive.

All the fragrances are based on the distinctive scents in Capri's location, using flowers and natural plant materials.

Today the business has grown to stores all over the world, but Capri is the only place to see the original factory. In addition to perfumes, the product line has expanded to body creams, scents for the home, diffusers, candles, soaps, sachets, bath accessories, and more. Special products for men are available, such as a shaving soap bowl encased in olive wood and accompanying aftershave. The little scent pots outside the shop are a nice touch, giving prospective customers the opportunity to preview the fragrances. Since time always seems to elude me in Italy, I must include a visit to Carthusia on my next visit to Capri.

***

Whenever I shop in Italy, I like to talk to the people, especially since most shops are run by families. I learn a lot about the culture and the lifestyle of the locals that way. These are real people, the locals who work hard and take pride in everything they do. They do it with a smile and in my experience, they always seem happy to engage in conversation. It's never "just business."

Longano Restaurant in Capri

Today is not my first time visiting Capri. I've been to this amazing island twice before. One of the most gorgeous places on earth, Capri can be touristy, especially during the day as it swells with crowds of cruise ship passengers known as day-trippers. On both of my previous trips, I must admit, I was one of them.

Traveling alone today, I do not need to revisit sites from my previous excursions. Today's agenda involves returning for the sheer purpose of dining at a restaurant that bears my name, Ristorante Longano. Eager to start my day, I'm waiting on the dock ahead of the scheduled departure, and at 9:30 a.m. I board the boat to Capri at the port of Amalfi.

This ferry ride is especially enjoyable for me on this balmy October day in 2014, for two reasons. First, I love to be near the water, no matter where I am; and second, the coastal scenery is spectacular beyond my wildest imagination. Experiencing the ride in person surpasses any photos or written accounts. A quick stop in Positano to pick up and drop off passengers guarantees a wondrous perspective and another photo opportunity for me. The entire town is visible when approaching by boat, and it is much different from any other view. So even though I am not visiting Positano this trip, I am fortunate enough to be able to see this delightful town on a perfect-weather day.

By 10:45 a.m. the boat arrives at Marina Grande, the larger of Capri's two ports, and this time, rather than take a taxi, I decide to ride the *funicolare* (cable car) to the center of Capri. A one-way ticket costs €1.80, and I can see the ticket booth to the far right of the pier. After some confusion, I realize that I must purchase a ticket prior to getting into line for the *funicolare*. Waiting at least twenty minutes in the queue makes me wonder whether the €5 taxi fare would have been a better idea, but it's too late now. After spending five days in Naples last week with the experienced Tina from Discover Napoli Destinations, I now know that this entire area — Naples, Capri, the Amalfi Coast — is all built on tufa stone, from lava, so unique modes of transportation, like a *funicolare*, are essential ways to move from lower to higher elevations.

The ride on this cable car provides a pleasant and quick alternative for navigating around these steep elevations. Now that I've reached the center of Capri, I need to try to accomplish a specific task before I look for Ristorante Longano. More than a nuisance, my camera battery is dead, fully exhausted, end-of-life. The two photo shops in Amalfi are out of stock for the battery I need, so I'm hopeful the upscale town of Capri might have exactly what I'm looking for.

After checking at both shops, I have no luck. I could kick myself, because my son Brian always reminds me to be sure to take an extra camera battery. I know he's right, and after this frustrating episode I will always have a spare on future trips. At least I have a camera on my iPhone, and at eight megapixels, the photos are fairly good quality, although I will have to do without a lot of the features on my Nikon Coolpix. Flexibility is the name of the game when traveling.

After I wander around a bit and shoot a few photos, I am back in the *piazzetta* (small square) where I expect to find Via Longano. In Independence, the suburb of Cleveland, Ohio, where I grew up, a street bearing my maiden name of Longano also exists. Longano Drive is actually named after my paternal grandfather, who owned and developed the land. This street in Capri is not connected to my family, from what I'm told. Still, knowing about the street and the restaurant is pretty cool, and I'm excited to be here.

From the restaurant's website, I remember a photo with a hand-drawn arrow alongside some simple instructions for locating the place. "Ristorante Pizzeria Longano is located just meters from Capri's main piazza. Just pass under the archway next to the City Hall and we are on the left." I'm also glad I took note that the restaurant closes on Tuesdays and is not open between 3:00 p.m. and 7:00 p.m.

Just under the arch, attached to the wall, is a rectangular ceramic sign, hand-painted in shades of blue, green, and yellow, indicating that this alleyway is Via Longano. A second sign hangs nearby and bears a story in Italian and English that seems to explain the origin of the street's name.

Dal Greco "longones" grandi pietre La strada poggia e si snoda lungo il primo tratto della muraglia megalitica construita con grossi blocchi i sodomici nel XIII secolo a.C.forse dai mitici Teleboi.

From ancient Greek "longones" (large stones used for the building of walls) The street rests on and runs along the megalithic walls built in the 8th cent. B.C., with huge blocks maybe by the mythical Teleboi.

I don't realize it now, but later, after doing some research, I learn that the first people to settle on Capri were ancient Greeks, known as Teleboi, who arrived on this island in the eighth century B.C.

Next to that sign are almost twenty more colorful ceramic signs listing each of the restaurants and hotels in this direction. Seeing the blue decorative sign that reads "Ristorante Pizzeria Longano" prompts a smile on my face, and my pulse races a bit from the excitement. As I wander down this curving passageway, too narrow for cars to maneuver, I spot the restaurant. An espresso-colored awning with letters in light tan announces "Pizzereria Ristorante Longano da Tarantino." I'm not sure about the *da Tarantino* part, but this must be the place. Another awning simply reads, "Ristorante Longano."

As I walk through the inviting entrance, I am only a foot away from the *pizzaiolo*, who is hard at work in front of a wood-fired oven. I always enjoy watching someone making pizza in Italy, so I don't mind waiting to be shown to my table. Wearing a clean white T-shirt and round, white hat, he smiles at me and nods, and I return the gesture. The counter is lightly covered with a yellow, powdery dust, what appears to be fine corn meal. I love the authenticity, and especially that the man is Italian. So often in America, and sometimes even in Italy in the bigger cities, a pizza shop advertises authentic Italian pizza but the pizza maker is from a foreign country. Disappointing, but a sign of the economic times, I guess.

After mentioning to the hostess that my name is Longano, I ask for the owner. She informs me that he is not here, and I'm surprised when she explains that the owner's name is not Longano. When I ask about the restaurant's name, she clarifies that the restaurant is named for the street, Via Longano, rather than the other way around. That makes sense, so now the question is solved. I'm happy to be shown to my table, with no further need to meet the owner.

Lunch here proves to be a pleasant experience, mainly because she seats me at a table next to a window with a stunning, unobstructed view stretching all the way to the sea. I'm lucky to have arrived early in the day before all the tables become occupied for lunch. Since I want to relish this special experience, I plan on absorbing my surroundings and living *la dolce vita*, so I take my time to peruse the menu. With such a huge selection of pizza, I understand why so many reviews on Trip Advisor credit this as the best pizza in Capri. More than twenty-five pizza options grace the menu, beginning with *focaccia con pomodorini* (raised pizza with fresh tomatoes), at €5.50; the classic *margherita* pizza at €7.00; and *frutti di mare* (seafood pizza), the most expensive at €13.00. I've come to expect that, just as in every Italian restaurant here, an entire pizza is served as the meal for one person. *How is it that Italians never gain weight?*

I'm not famished, so I decide to have the spaghetti with *pomodori* and *basilico* and ask if they can serve it with penne pasta instead of the classic spaghetti. I'm delighted when my waiter informs me in perfect English that he'd be happy to do so. No salad for me, just some *acqua naturale* and bread. After I order, I stand up to gaze out the expansive window and take in the breathtaking view of Capri. Naturally, I snap a few shots with my phone, and they will have to do. I feel happy that "my" restaurant is such a good one. I think I'd be disappointed if Ristorante Longano had turned out to be only mediocre.

Today I don't mind eating alone, even when I see the other patrons wander in as couples or families. I am savoring the moment as well as the food, which tastes delicious and warrants the high reviews and coveted Trip Advisor certificate of excellence. My food choice is perfect, and I'm not able to finish it all. I can't even imagine how I could eat an entire pizza. But after eyeing the other patrons' pizzas, I think maybe next time I'll have one myself. I'd like to try the Longano pizza, which is described as white pizza with Parma ham, arugula, and shaved Parmesan cheese.

This restaurant features a special "menu of the day" that offers a limited selection of a first and second course, vegetable, and dessert, all for €16, including the *coperto* (cover charge). A ten percent service charge is not included and neither are the beverages. For Capri, the prices are quite reasonable. And now the story behind the *da Tarantino* on the awning is revealed. Since 1987, Giovanni Tarantino has been welcoming diners here, continuing his family tradition of warm hospitality and excellent food at fair prices. I know I'll be back.

After lunch I still have some time to browse and window-shop a bit in Capri before my return ferry trip. No pressure, since I have nothing I need to purchase this time. Two hours after I arrived here, I take the same *funicolare* back to the marina, and for this ride a line is nonexistent. I am early for the return boat to Amalfi, so I decide to have a gelato near the waterfront at a place where I can use the restroom and connect to Wi-Fi. The €8 cost for two scoops of *amarena* gelato is pricey but typical for Capri and well worth it for me.

Bar Corallo is the perfectly positioned place to kill time and people-watch. Its outdoor seating area fronts Marina Grande, so I will be able to see my ferry when it arrives and can then walk the short distance to board in time. I like the congenial woman who waits on me here. We strike up a conversation, and I learn that she and her husband are the owners of a jewelry shop across the street. She proudly tells me that they sell the famous Capri watches and, good salesperson that she is, invites me to have a look. After I finish my gelato and have had enough time to use Wi-Fi, I check out the shop but don't buy anything. Instead, I return to my conveniently positioned table and relax a little longer, enjoying the warm sun and the fairy-tale view.

***

After I arrive back in Amalfi, I fight the urge to lie down in my hotel room and crash for the day and decide to investigate whether the cathedral is open. Known by various names, the Amalfi Cathedral is also called St. Andrew's Cathedral, Duomo di Amalfi, and Duomo di Sant'Andrea. Only a five-minute walk from the dock, I arrive at the central piazza and this grand church. My timing can't be much better, since a sign indicates it's open this afternoon from 5:00 p.m. until 7:00 p.m., and I'm glad for the opportunity. The cathedral's dramatic location requires climbing a steep flight of sixty-two steps to reach the entrance. Once there, I'm impressed by the spectacular view of the amazing piazza below. I understand a local legend warns couples not to climb these steps holding hands, or else they will never get married. I love hearing about these ancient stories in Amalfi.

Originally built in the ninth century, the Cathedral of St. Andrew underwent massive renovations several centuries ago and today is considered a marvelous example of diverse architectural styles. While its predominant original style was Arab-Norman Romanesque, its later restorations include those elements as well as byzantine and gothic designs. The striking bell tower to the left features an ornate dome, including the cupola and four turrets adorned in brilliant green and yellow majolica tiles. I find the dome's appearance striking. With the relics of St. Andrew the Apostle in its crypt, the inside of this cathedral is as impressive as its façade. I'm struck by its elegant beauty. This cathedral extends to a beautiful cloister and even another church attached to it, but I will leave those explorations for another day.

For now, I'm heading back to my comfortable hotel room to rest and relax. Every hour of every day doesn't need to be filled with excursions and activities. Tonight's luminous full moon shines with such brilliance and provides me with a clear view of the sea from my balcony. *Serenity.*

I Drove on the Amalfi Coast

As attractive as the Amalfi Coast is, this place has not always been a touristy area. After doing some research and learning more about Amalfi's history, I understand much more. During the ninth century, the town of Amalfi was one of the first Italian maritime republics, rivaling Pisa, Genoa, and Venice as a naval power and trader with the east. Amalfi even had its own currency called the taro. In 1073, Amalfi fell under Norman control and was later annexed by King Roger II of Sicily. Attacked by the Pisans in the twelfth century, Amalfi continued to decline. In the fourteenth century, when the plague caused most of its inhabitants to die and a storm destroyed the port, the ships, and most of the town, the kingdom of Naples took over the rule of the small, sleepy fishing village that Amalfi had become.

Until the nineteenth century, the Amalfi Coast remained isolated geographically, but things were about to change. When Giuseppe Bonaparte, King of Naples, visited the coast, he became captivated by its beauty and decided he'd like to build a road from Naples to Amalfi to make it easier to access these towns. Although the road was started in 1816, it was not completed until 1854, after being formally commissioned by Ferdinand II, the Bourbon King of Naples. I always say nothing happens fast in Italy, and this was true in the past as well.

Writers, poets, artists, and other travelers began to discover this beautiful area, and during a visit to Amalfi, the American poet Henry Longfellow was inspired by his time there and wrote a poem titled "Amalfi" in 1875. Today the Amalfi Drive is believed to be the most scenic and spectacular road in Europe, known throughout the world for its sheer beauty and breathtaking views.

Officially known as Strada Statale 163, or SS 163 Amalfitana, the Amalfi Drive is also called the Costiera Amalfitana (Amalfi Coast) Road. Originally built by the Romans, the two-lane asphalt road is five meters wide. Hugging the coast, the serpentine motorway connects the seaside towns of the Amalfi Coast. Part of the road runs along the sea, as in Maiori, and other sections precariously hug the sea cliff edge hundreds of meters above the shoreline. Since it was built at such a steep angle, the road zigzags back and forth, with railings only at certain places, contributing to the white-knuckle driving experience. And yes, I am going to drive it. Round convex mirrors are installed at some of the hairpin turns so drivers can see around the bend ahead. Am I scared? No, but I'm cautious.

I recall reading horror stories of travelers who became dizzy and nauseated riding the SITA bus along this stretch of road. I'm not prone to vertigo or dizziness, so my past experiences on the bus rides were good. I also recall saying that I'd never attempt to drive this road myself, but life is full of changes, and this is the year I'm taking on the challenge. I'm driving the Amalfi Coast Road, and I'm kind of excited.

The year is 2012, and my friend Sue and I are traveling by car from Salerno to Rome. Since we have time to spare, I suggest driving to Maiori and spending some time relaxing by the sea. In May the weather is great, and Sue says she's game. Before we check out of our hotel in the coastal town of Pontecagnano Faiano near Salerno, I have the pleasure of meeting Gaetano, one of the young owners of the four-star Hotel Olimpico.

When I mention that we plan to drive to the Amalfi Coast and, from there, continue on to Rome, he informs us about a marathon that is happening today in Salerno. "All the streets will be closed to traffic in the center of town. You don't want to get mixed up in that. Let me show you a better way to go, so you can bypass Salerno," he suggests in a helpful way. He provides a map with detailed instructions for getting to the Amalfi Coast Road by going around Salerno. We chat a bit and I relate the story about my driving experience and construction delays yesterday between Sicily and Salerno. Suffice it to say that between getting lost and dealing with detours, police, and road crews, I'd like to forget about the ten hours of frustration on Italy's roads.

Grateful for his local expertise, I have to laugh when he tells me that the *autostrada* (major highway with tolls) from Sicily to Salerno is the worst one in Italy and is always under construction. With immense pride, he shares that the freeway between here and Rome is a much better one and, in fact, the best in Italy. Again, I smile to myself when I hear this last phrase. I can't count how many times I've heard Italians describe something as the best of something, no matter what they're talking about. I think it's a culturally accepted expression.

At least I can expect today's ride to be an improvement over yesterday's, and since this is my last day of driving in Italy this trip, I'm happy. Sue and I load our luggage into our white Mercedes rental car, and I drive toward the A3 Autostrada. From Gaetano's instructions, I understand that when we reach Vietri sul Mare, I will be able to access the Amalfi Coast Road.

Everything so far is smooth sailing, and Gaetano's directions are perfect. As long as I follow the signs that direct me toward Costiera Amalfitana, I know I'm in the right spot. Well, I guess it's too good to be true, because all of a sudden I end up going the wrong way on a one-way road. Fortunately, traffic is light, and I'm able to correct my error without any problem. One other minor glitch adds to the adventure when I miss a turn and am forced to drive a few extra miles up a hill into the next town and turn around. This detour includes paying a toll in both directions, adding to the frustration. I guess things could be worse, so I'm trying not to let this hiccup get in the way of a good time. Soon I see the exit for Vietri, turn off, and am now driving on the scenic Costiera Amalfitana.

Since this stretch of the Amalfi Coast Road is not new to me, having traveled it by bus last year, I sort of know what to expect, although the trip seems longer now that I'm the driver. Today is Sunday and traffic is not heavy, so I appreciate the luxury of being able to take my time and drive slowly without feeling rushed or stressed by too many other drivers riding my rear bumper.

Memories from years past flood my mind as I recall trips out west in the States, driving our family van through some of the national parks in California. Known for their numerous switchbacks and s-bends, those drives are much like this one.

With its high cliffs and rock formations all the way down to the sea, the Amalfi Coast exudes majesty and magnificence. I'm beginning to think this has to be my favorite spot in Italy.

Once I drive past the town of Vietri sul Mare, I see a place where I'm able to pull off the road to park, so I can capture a photo of this lovely place far below. The natural lighting this morning is radiant and I'm pleased. While Sue waits in the car for me, I compose what I perceive to be a perfect image and shoot just two photos, satisfied with this digital souvenir from Vietri. In less than five minutes, I return to the car and continue to drive in the direction of Maiori.

In a little while, we reach the seaside town of Cetara, a tiny fishing village. I like how the road rolls right through the center of town, and I make a mental note to return one day and spend more time exploring this charming community. "Isn't this town cute, Sue? I always wanted to come here, and in fact thought about it when I suggested driving to the Amalfi Coast on our way to Rome."

"Yeah, I like it. You can see the people in their everyday lives going about their business. I love the laundry hanging out too," Sue says.

"I know. I'd like to come back another time. I thought Maiori might be a better option since I'm familiar with it. I know they have a lovely promenade along the sea, and we can sit and relax there."

"That sounds great," Sue says, "especially after that grueling day of driving yesterday, getting lost at the port and then getting stopped by the Italian police."

"Oh, don't remind me, please. I could have done without that police situation." I'm laughing now but yesterday was another story. "I'm not afraid to admit I was more than a little nervous."

Sue is referring to a surprise traffic stop when the Italian police pulled me over for crossing a solid yellow line to pass a slow-moving vehicle. I don't know what happened to my mind, but I didn't even realize I had done anything wrong. I'm fortunate he gave me a break, issuing only a verbal warning after reviewing my documents. Driving in Italy challenges a traveler from the States like myself.

This drive today is pleasant and I feel in command of the car. I can tell from her reactions that the continual turns are not so much fun for Sue in the passenger seat, so I'm thankful she is a good sport and doesn't complain. Eventually we get closer to Maiori, and I welcome the chance to get out of the car and relax. Driving into the town, I remember the layout well from my five days here last year. The beach is about a mile long, so I know not to drive too far, or else I'll be going up the hill to the next town, Minori. Plenty of parking spots are available on the street, so I choose one and we get out of the car.

"That feels good after sitting for so long," Sue says.

"I agree. I'm so happy to be here." Today's partly cloudy sky does not deter us one bit. A slight breeze along the seafront makes everything wonderful. Both of us love the water, and we cross the street and walk along the promenade, soaking in the refreshing sea air and ambience. At Lido Bussola, an outdoor beach bar, we find plenty of empty tables and chairs and sit down.

"How does a cappuccino sound?" I say to Sue.

"Perfect. I'll take two," she replies.

We both saunter up to the counter and order three cappuccinos from Antonio for the modest price of one euro fifty cents per cup. How about that for a deal? Back at our beachfront table, we sip our cappuccinos and unwind from

157

the drive. The tranquility of this coast almost mesmerizes me, while providing the perfect antidote for any stress. I think Henry Wadsworth Longfellow's poem "The Secret of the Sea" sums up my thoughts at this moment. "My soul is full of longing for the secret of the sea, and the heart of the great ocean sends a thrilling pulse through me." *Did he write that for me?*

After ten or fifteen minutes, I'm in the mood for some gelato. Sue declines, but I walk across the street to the gelato shop, where two scoops cost two euros, another bargain. I choose *amarena*, made with fresh black cherries, and pistachio. I savor this sweet treat, since I know it will likely be my last gelato in Italy before I fly home tomorrow. Once I return to Lido Bussola, we both sit a while longer and appreciate the idyllic setting and the luxury of doing nothing. Near the end of a long trip, bliss is the best way to describe the feeling I have. Rome is only two or three hours driving distance from here, barring any problems, and we have all day to get there.

Sue and I stroll along the promenade again before leaving Maiori, and suddenly we hear a voice calling us. We both turn to see Antonio running toward us, and he is waving something in the air. When Sue sees him, she realizes that he has her wallet.

"I must have left it on the table when we had the cappuccino," she says. "Grazie, Antonio." How considerate of Antonio to run after us to return her wallet. Do you think this kind of honesty and goodness happens everywhere? Just another reason to fall in love with these towns in Italy.

Leaving Maiori and heading to Rome necessitates more driving along the Amalfi Coast, basically retracing our steps until we reach the entrance to the *autostrada*. From there, the rest of the trip should be a straight ride to Rome on the best *autostrada* in Italy, according to Gaetano's description. Time proves his words to ring true, and we arrive at Rome's airport, where we return the car with no problem. This process turns out to be much simpler than the fiasco that occurred when renting it the first day. Chaos and inefficiency by the personnel at the rental car desk in Rome is the only way to describe my aggravation that day. I remember waiting forty-five minutes to speak to an agent, only to discover there was no record of a reservation. We left with a larger car than we needed or wanted and then had not received the ticket necessary to open the exit gate from the parking area. This required a return inside to retrieve it. I clearly recall the entire situation, which lasted over two hours.

After checking the mileage on the odometer, I can now proclaim that I have achieved 1,200 miles of driving experience in Italy in a five- day period. For my first time driving here, I am satisfied with my performance, although the decision to drive from Rome to Sicily and back in five days is not very economical. In fact, in hindsight, I realize it's stupid. With so many low-cost flight options available within Italy, I can purchase a round-trip ticket to Sicily for much less than the cost of a rental car, tolls, and diesel fuel combined. In the future, that is exactly what I plan to do. Live and learn.

Staying in Amalfi

It's May of 2014, and anyone who knows me realizes that I enjoy travel planning almost as much as I enjoy the trip. Well, not quite, but I do like figuring out my own itinerary when I go to Italy, and I also like the idea of finding the best deals I can. In fact, this is how my next trip to Italy materializes.

My original thought is to go to Italy next spring, but now my visit shifts to this October. Since I love Italy so much and never stop wishing I could be there, my desire strengthens the more I hear friends talking about their upcoming trips to *bella Italia*. I make a deal with myself to go to Italy this fall, but only if I find a fantastic airfare, since that is one of the most costly parts of a trip to Italy—airfare and accommodations. Well, I find a nonstop airfare from JFK Airport in New York to Malpensa Airport in Milan for the incredible price of $643 round trip, half the cost of my last transatlantic flight. Elated, I waste no time making a decision about returning to Italy sooner rather than later. And I justify my decision as the perfect gift to myself to celebrate my upcoming retirement from nursing after a forty-four-year career. No longer needing to worry about vacation requests this fall, I choose the time frame of three weeks and book my flight.

Researching destinations and deals, I spend a couple of months working out an itinerary which includes the Amalfi Coast. I'm curious whether it's better to take a train or a cheap flight within Italy to travel from the north to the south. After perusing the online airline search engines, I discover that an inexpensive hour-and-a-half flight from Milan to Naples is a better deal than a four-and-a-half-hour train ride. Not only is the shortened time preferable, but the difference in cost is negligible, even factoring in the €7.50 price for the Malpensa Express bus ride to the airport in Milan.

I remember debating with myself which town to use as a hub for a vacation on the Amalfi Coast. Since I'm traveling solo and not renting a car, I must rely on public transportation. Easy access to that transportation is one of the important criteria when travel planning. Having made Sorrento a hub on my first trip to this coast, I decide to book a hotel stay in the town of Amalfi for four nights. Never having stayed in Amalfi before, I hope to explore the city on foot and savor its flavor at a slow pace. From there I can take day trips to other places on the coast as well.

Opting for more luxurious accommodations this trip, I select a hotel that looks as if it will more than meet my expectations. After I complete the hotel reservation through Booking.com, I scan the hotel's website and discover the room price to be cheaper than the price on the travel fare aggregator website. Dismayed, I think about options, aware that the reservation is refundable. I make a short phone call to Italy via Skype, and a pleasant English-speaking receptionist named Vittoria answers and listens to my dilemma. I am euphoric when she informs me that she is happy to book a reservation for me at the hotel's discounted rate. She even reassures me that it is refundable up to four days ahead. Sometimes it pays to book directly with a hotel. And guess what? The cost of four nights in this glamorous hotel ends up to be only $33 more than the cost of five nights in the spartan monastery in Maiori where I stayed a few years ago.

***

Hotel Residence, a four-star hotel right in the heart of Amalfi, is my home for the next four days and nights. With a view of the Mediterranean Sea, I'm thrilled with my choice, even though I'm splurging on the accommodation. So much for an economical vacation. After all, I am celebrating.

Breakfast on the hotel's large terrace this morning can't be any better. With a view of the cerulean blue Tyrrhenian Sea and the beach below, I'm relaxed and happy, as the warm sun streams in. I could be happy just sitting here all day sipping my cappuccino and enjoying the Italian pastries and fresh fruit from the breakfast buffet.

Converted into a hotel in the 1950s and totally renovated in 2010, this eighteenth-century, former aristocratic *palazzo* (palace) presents a mix of modern and classic decor. As I walk down the spiral staircase with its wrought iron railing, I take time to appreciate the antique artwork and dark wood furniture in what might have once been a parlor. The furnishings in this well-appointed hotel contribute to the luxury and welcoming atmosphere. My room is also lovely, and I especially enjoy my private balcony where I sit and write after I unwind from the day. In these luxurious surroundings I am content beyond any aspirations.

No longer the powerful capital of the Duchy of Amalfi, the town of Amalfi remains a busy nucleus today. Ferries and buses whisk travelers to and from Amalfi to locations along the Amalfi Coast and the Gulf of Napoli. Without a train station to service this city or the other villages and towns along the coast, Amalfi is the transportation center, which is one of my reasons for selecting this place as a hub. Along the waterfront are the ferry docks, bus station, and parking lot, and during the day and into the evening the SITA buses arrive and depart for points along the Amalfi Coast. So from here, a day excursion to Sorrento, Capri, Positano, Salerno, or other points up and down the coast is easy to arrange.

I love Amalfi's evening and nighttime vibe. The town feels alive, and outdoor establishments are filled with patrons. Late into the night, lovers share an intimate meal by candlelight at an outdoor trattoria on one of the narrow side streets, and travelers delight in the warm evening air as they dine in one of the countless restaurants near Piazza del Duomo.

This evening I'd like to find a quiet place, though, away from the noise in the main square, where I can have a leisurely dinner. On the recommendation of the front desk manager, I head toward the bustling Piazza del Duomo and the Amalfi Cathedral of St. Andrew with its huge staircase. Hundreds of people fill the street tonight in this summerlike weather. Turning left, I walk up a steep alley until I come upon the tiny Piazza del Dogi. I arrive at Ristorante L'Abside, ten minutes after leaving my hotel.

At first glance, I don't see any empty tables outside, which is no surprise since it's nine fifteen in the evening, typical Italian dinner time. The lovely hostess asks me to wait a minute or two, and she returns and seats me inside, just until an outside table becomes available. I don't mind at all, and within a few more minutes, she returns to escort me to *un tavolo per uno* (a table for one) outside. The ambience is perfect in this temperate climate where a scarf might not even be needed this evening. The waiters and waitresses speak English, and I overhear a lot of English conversation from visitors with British accents. A quick look at the menu and I know what I'm having. A glass of prosecco, some *acqua naturale*, and homemade ravioli with a green salad is exactly what I need.

In the meantime, I'm immersed in the atmosphere. This piazza is more like a courtyard, enclosed by two-, three-, and four-story buildings in various shades of white and pastels. Based on the laundry drying on the balcony railings, I assume locals live on the upper floors. Other restaurants with outdoor seating are also located in the charming square. This piazza is like a one-stop shopping place. A deli-sized *supermercato* and a *farmacia* line the square amid other businesses and apartments. Later I learn that this unique square was once home to the Doge and other nobility, hence its name.

Dinner is delicious and I'm in no hurry. This seems like heaven to me, and I already predict that the next four days are going to be perfect. My plan here is to relax and enjoy Amalfi, maybe visit the nearby town of Ravello, and take the boat to Capri for an afternoon. I like not being tied to a strict itinerary.

***

Today, on the advice of an Italian Twitter follower, I decide to check out the ancient Arsenale della Repubblica, located close to the Amalfi beachfront. This ancient, well-preserved shipyard, dating back to the Middle Ages, is the place where trading vessels were once built during the heyday of this former powerful republic. The pointed-arch stone entrance with its high ceilings creates quite an impression on first view. After I pay the admission fee of two euros, I'm left to my own discretion and am told to browse at leisure. This place is now a museum that showcases the naval history of Amalfi and also doubles as an event venue. The musical *Amalfi* is advertised to be performed here.

Dimly lit and tiny, the Arsenal Museum provides a respite from shopping and its cool temperature a refreshing break from the outdoors. One of the most interesting exhibits is the compass display. I also notice the original gold coins, the *tari*, on display. From the descriptions posted, I learn that some local shops make and sell jewelry with these *tari*.

Antique nautical instruments, costumes worn during a maritime regatta, and the original maritime code, the Tabula Amalphitana, are featured here. Models of ships and a row-barge used in the ancient historical regatta are also part of this interesting collection. The Regatta of the Ancient Maritime Republics is a competition held each year and pits the crews of these four cities against each other: Amalfi, Genoa, Pisa, and Venice. The competition rotates among the cities, so every four years the event occurs in Amalfi. The next time Amalfi will host is in the year 2020.

Fascinated, I make my way around, reading the exhibits' information which is carefully displayed in English and Italian. Forty-five minutes later, I'm back outside and take a stroll on the long pier, where I can see the ferries dropping off passengers and the local fishing boats leaving the dock. A few people are in the water close to shore, and some young boys are kicking a soccer ball around. Life is good.

One place of interest here that I neglect to visit is the Museo della Carta, or the Paper Museum. I might like to include a stop there on my next trip. This museum is located in one of the original fourteenth-century paper mills up the hill from the town center. During one of my walks in that direction, I notice the sign for the paper mill, but without knowing how far it is, I don't continue up that way. Now I learn that the walk is only ten minutes uphill from the cathedral.

I think a visit to a museum that highlights the paper-making tradition of Amalfi would be interesting as well as educational. From what I understand, for only four euros, a guide explains the paper-making process during a twenty-five-minute tour of this ancient paper mill. The museum contains the equipment and machinery, restored to working condition, that the artisans used to make paper by hand centuries ago. On exhibition are the wooden mauls that are operated by a hydraulic wheel. A press that removes excess water from the paper and a printing machine are in use, and visitors can engage in an interactive experience of making paper themselves. In the eighteenth century, when Amalfi had fourteen paper mills, production was at its height. I wish now that I had explored the museum, because I love to watch artisans at work, especially in a tradition that is almost a lost art.

Today, only one working paper mill, Cartiera Amatruda, still exists in Amalfi. The mill produces handmade paper, envelopes, and watermarked cards using traditional techniques. These items can be purchased in local shops, and they can even be ordered online. The Amatruda paper mill is situated in the ancient Mill Valley high above the center of Amalfi, and it is attached to a bridge over the Canneto River. The oldest part of the building dates back to the fifteenth century, when the Amatruda family began their paper manufacturing tradition. I'd love to see this old mill on the river and the surrounding countryside which even has a waterfall.

***

As I wander by myself this evening, I savor the sweetness of a gelato while I stroll up Via Lorenzo d'Amalfi and listen to the dulcet sounds of Italian music as it emanates from a lovely *ristorante*. Noticing two diners at an intimate outdoor table as they indulge in a slice of torta d'Amalfi (a traditional lemon sponge cake), I smile to myself. And when I walk past two lovers sipping Costa d'Amalfi Rosso while they gaze into each other's eyes, I secretly toast them. I am a romantic at heart, no doubt about it.

Amalfi is enchanting, especially at night. I would be deceiving myself if I didn't admit that I'm a bit jealous on evenings like this. As much as I enjoy traveling solo and the independence of wandering about on my own, I sometimes dream about how different the experience would be if I were with someone special, someone I love. When I see couples holding hands at an intimate outdoor table or strolling arm in arm along the seashore, I wonder what that might be like for me. A picturesque location like the pristine Amalfi Coast, celebrated in words by poets, authors, and screenwriters, and depicted in art by cinematographers, artists, and photographers, is the quintessential romantic setting.

As I allow my dreams to expand, I can envision how we'd hunt for sea glass on the beach together, dine in a Michelin-starred restaurant with a view of the sea, and sleep in a hotel on the beach, where the waves would lull us to sleep. What fun it would be to ride the SITA bus around the winding coastline with him, get off at one of the coastal villages, and simply wander together with no set agenda. Sharing a gelato, a glass of wine, a cappuccino, or an *aperitivo* would be that much better with my love.

Who knows what tomorrow brings? I remember a wise friend telling me to keep an open mind. I believe in carpe diem; to seize the day and make the most of the present makes sense to me, and this is how I live my life. So far, I have no complaints. I'm happy and I'm making things happen. When friends wistfully tell me they'd like to travel as much as I do, I have one piece of advice for them: "Carpe diem. Make it happen. You are in control of your life. If you want something bad enough, do what it takes for your dream to come true."

I think of myself as an optimist, a positive person. I believe negativity is useless and accomplishes nothing. Hanging around with negative people can drag one down, so I try not to spend much time like that. None of us knows the future, and life is short. My thought is to enjoy today because everything can certainly change in an instant. I realize that some situations in life are out of my control, but I believe I do have a choice about how I deal with them, and that makes all the difference between a positive and a negative outlook. By embracing life, I stay happy.

I'm reminded of these inspiring words by an unknown author and often mistakenly attributed to Mark Twain, but I like them nonetheless:

Life is short, break the rules, forgive quickly, kiss slowly, love truly, laugh uncontrollably, and never regret anything that made you smile. Twenty years from now, you will be more disappointed by the things you didn't do than by the ones you did. So throw off the bowlines. Sail away from the safe harbor. Catch the trade winds in your sails. Explore. Dream. Discover.

Let's see what comes next.

Staying in Positano

In my wildest dreams, I never thought I'd be fortunate enough to stay in Positano, the jewel of the Amalfi Coast. Known as the vacation spot for the rich and famous, the expense of staying in one of the hotels here always seemed out of reach for me. But in June of 2015, my impossible dream transforms into a reality when my good friend and travel partner arranges a stay at a family owned, beachfront, three-star hotel for an affordable rate, split between us. I can hardly believe it, but after reviewing the information and photos available on the internet, this accommodation looks perfect. I am excited and can hardly imagine what spending five glorious days and nights in Positano will be like.

My travel adventure begins in Venice when I meet up with two passionate Italy travel bloggers, Victoria De Maio and Susan Nelson, whom I know from social media and consider friends. From there, Susan and I join Victoria for the next ten days on her Puglia Experience, which turns out to be far more than I could anticipate. I highly recommend it to both new and seasoned travelers. Following the custom group experience, the three of us extend our trip together to the seaside town of Polignano a Mare, followed by Matera, in the Basilicata region, and end the three-week adventure in the relaxing Amalfi Coast town of Positano.

We ride along the scenic Amalfi Coast Road with Michele, our competent driver, at the wheel, and my heart skips a beat as soon as I recognize the approach to Positano, the city with the homes that appear to jut out from the cliffs high above the sea. "Oh my God, isn't this gorgeous? I love it here," I say to Susan and Victoria.

"Yes, it's so beautiful. I'm really glad we decided to end our trip here. I so need to relax," Victoria gushes.

"I know what you're saying. I can't wait to walk along the beach," Susan adds.

Choosing this beautiful seaside location as the last stop on this Italy experience is ideal, because by now I look forward to unwinding in a comfortable hotel with a view of the water. Our entertaining Italian driver bids us arrivederci when he drops the three of us and our luggage at a parking garage in the upper part of Positano. Vehicles are not permitted to navigate any farther down, where the streets narrow into pedestrian walkways which soon disappear and are replaced by staircases and inclined paths. We take turns giving Michele a hug and are greeted by two muscular, young, friendly porters from Hotel Pupetto, our beachfront hotel. With utmost proficiency and expertise, they distribute all of our bags onto two wagons and point us in the direction we need to go to reach the hotel. One tells us he will meet us there with our bags. "Just keep going down" is the only instruction he shares.

We're grateful not to transport the bags ourselves, although none of us has any idea what awaits us next. Excitement reigns as we eagerly begin our downhill trek to

171

the beach. I'm carrying a heavy bag with a laptop inside, since I didn't want to leave it with the porters, and I'm regretting my decision the father we walk.

Little do we know that we will traverse more than three hundred steps before we eventually arrive at the hotel, hot and sticky in the middle of this summer day. June on the Amalfi Coast seems to be hotter than normal. In reality, most of Italy is experiencing record-high temperatures this season. I'm glad to be dressed in casual capris and sandals.

"How much longer is this walk?" I ask my fellow travelers, who are ahead of me. I'm breathing hard and trying to keep up. Frustrated and hot, I yell to Victoria, who is almost out of my sight by now, "Victoria, how far is this place?"

"It's on the beach, so just follow us," she yells back.

Susan, who is thin and very fit and enjoys hiking, seems to take it in stride but also questions the number of additional steps we are facing. Waiting for me, she offers to take my heavy, oversized purse, and I'm grateful for the help.

"Thank you, Susan. I need to get in better shape, that's for sure." Cursing myself for not losing the weight I wanted to release before this trip, I'm praying we don't have much farther to go.

Victoria adds, "I'll be looking for a glass of vino when we get there, for sure." Despite the challenge, I feel certain we all know that the final destination will be relaxing.

As we draw closer to the hotel, I catch my first glimpse of the azure blue sea from the staircase, and now the downhill walk becomes worth all the effort and sweat! I am convinced this is where I long to be, and a sense of sheer joy bathes my body, as if to cleanse the moisture away. And the best part is, we have five days here.

To reach the hotel's reception desk we must walk along a stone path through a garden in full bloom, with aromatic lemon trees, glorious bougainvillea in hues of magenta and purple, huge snowball hydrangea flowers, and other tropical flora. I can smell the sweet aroma of the lemons hanging on vines intertwined on the pergola overhead.

As we make our way to the open-air reception area, I catch sight of the delightfully decorated, expansive terrace restaurant. Square tables covered in blue-and-white tablecloths are complemented by white wrought iron chairs with matching blue seat cushions and are set for the next meal. Ristorante Pupetto is part of the hotel, and with such an inviting atmosphere, I can guess exactly where Victoria's first glass of wine will be. The ceramic tile floors, in shades of terra-cotta and gray, balance the attractive design.

The terrace restaurant overlooks the wondrous Tyrrhenian Sea, where boats of all sizes are buoyed. What a gorgeous scene. *I could stay here forever!* "Victoria, this place is perfect. I'm so glad you found this hotel. I love it here already," I say.

The friendly, English-speaking hotel staff welcomes us, and the check-in process is easy. Since Susan made her decision to travel with us after the initial arrangements were made, her room is on another floor, but not far away from ours. We are escorted to our rooms up a double flight of steps, which seems like child's play after the walk from the parking area. Once I am inside the room, I find the luggage has been delivered, and now I can take a break and chill out. As soon as I walk out onto the balcony, I know that I'm in heaven. Nothing can be better than this moment.

For the next five nights this view belongs to me, and although I'm sharing the space with my friend, I anticipate how the rhythmic sounds of the soft waves will soothe me to sleep. My daydreams become my reality, and no further explanation is necessary as to why this is my favorite place in Italy. Positano casts a magical spell on anyone who's experienced her charm, and I'm certainly one of those people.

***

If you are one to believe in legends, the story goes that Positano was founded by Neptune, god of water and the sea. It was here that Neptune fell in love with the nymph Pasitea, the inspiration for the name of the town. Award-winning author John Steinbeck described Positano as the most perpendicular village in the world. And his words are accurate, since the houses and hotels are accessible only by long, winding stairways from sea level to a road high above the city. If you're not fond of exercise, then you'll resent all the staircases and inclines you have to traverse in this town. Yet, for me, the tremendous views along the way are so completely worth it. Positano is the perfect place to do nothing but relax.

After we get settled in our room and unpack, Victoria and I walk down the steps to meet Susan in the open-air terrace restaurant. We decide it's time to salute our travel journey with some prosecco, which I much prefer over wine. Just sitting at a table close to the sea and hearing the sounds of the gentle waves rolling back and forth is magical. Three good friends who love Italy can't ask for a better way to celebrate our arrival on the Amalfi Coast.

With no agenda, the freedom to experience *il dolce far niente* at this moment surpasses any planned excursion. I love that Italian phrase and sometimes when I travel, I forget to put it into practice. A way of life in Italy, this concept is an integral part of the Italian culture. The idea of doing nothing except enjoying the present moment is sometimes hard for an American to grasp, given our aggressive work ethic. Just giving myself permission to enjoy the passing of time and letting my thoughts wander is freeing. I'd like to make this more of a habit. To be able to embrace this mantra, where all that matters is living in the moment, reduces stress and pressure. Even if time slows just for a while, it's better than rush, rush, rush.

I have my own idea of the meaning of this popular phrase that fascinates me so much, but I like to hear what Italians think. When I ask my native Italian friends to share how they observe this tradition, their answers intrigue me.

My friend Marco from Venice describes the tradition as "enjoying life without working and being at peace with nature and oneself." Daniela from Rome reveals it's "to lay down on a sunny beach listening to the lapping of the sea with a fresh drink in my hand." Luisa from Florence tells me, "It's that short moment of relaxation and peace after a busy exciting day or time, and yet anticipating something even more exciting to come. A moment suspended among the pleasures of life." I like this thought a lot.

Michele from Lecce stays busy all the time and admits that he rarely practices this lifestyle, but when he does, it's in the form of reading, listening to his favorite music, or a walk on the beach with his dogs. I'm heartened to know that even some Italians don't always succeed in unplugging and doing nothing—not always an easy concept to embrace, but more than likely a healthier one, mentally as well as physically. My cousin Antonella, from Colle d'Anchise, says, "It means when the only thing you want to do is nothing, spend your time relaxing and doing nothing special." Piero from Florence shares several thoughts about *il dolce far niente*. He tells me it's "to relax, and do nothing . . . even thinking too hard," and it's "perfect in a small village sitting with friends outside the bar, but hardly exists for people who lead an average life in a city." He elaborates by saying, "We Italians are considered, I guess, a bit lazy, but able to enjoy life, and probably through *il dolce far niente* you become more creative." Some perspectives to ponder, for certain.

***

In the early evening, Susan, Victoria, and I decide to wander into the center of Positano. Hotel Pupetto is situated on the quiet Fornillo Beach, away from the busier main beach of Spiaggia Grande and the town center. The helpful Gabriella at the reception desk provides us with directions, saying it's only a ten-minute walk, and we head toward town. Ten minutes later, we still haven't reached our destination, and I'm thinking . . . *Were we just played or what?* And they always minimize the distance as they explain it with a smile, to make it a positive thing. Gotta love the Italians.

Let's see how long a walk this really is and if Gabriella's words ring true. The walkway to town passes through a tunnel and begins as an uphill climb along the sea, so naturally I have to stop to take photos. The gorgeous Fornillo Beach is below me, with its colorful orange and green umbrellas. An overlook just before a turn is the perfect point to capture this scene. A young couple sits quietly in this out-of-the-way place, sharing a special moment.

Continuing uphill, I'm still a bit skeptical about the ten-minute time frame, especially since I'm not as fit as I'd like to be. These uphill walks are another wake-up call to me, so I'm feeling the incline for sure.

In some places, more photo opportunities emerge, and in other spots, the views are obscured by high walls and trees, and the trail seems dark and private. A few travelers pass us as they walk in the opposite direction. We notice a couple of restaurants built into the rocky cliff wall, and stairs are required to reach their entrances. As the three of us keep moving along this paved path, we eventually reach a spot where I can see the town beneath us, and the fantastic postcard-like view is our reward. Framed by the limbs of a tree, the scene before my eyes forces me to take another photo or two—or ten. Thank goodness Victoria and Susan are also avid photographers, so they don't mind pausing to shoot photos.

I can envision how dreamy this walk might be at night under the moonlit sky. It's the perfect place for a romantic interlude, a lingering kiss or embrace with a special someone. Now the road winds downhill, contributing to an easier walk. Later I will learn that this corridor is named Via Positanesi d'America in honor of the many local residents who left Positano in the early nineteenth century to emigrate to America. I like the name.

Passing by the trendy Chez Black and Le Tre Sorelle, two of the most well-known restaurants on the beach, we arrive at Buca di Bacco, the most famous of these dining establishments, mostly due to the publicity it received in *Under the Tuscan Sun*. Just beneath the formal Buca di Bacco is another restaurant that is often mistaken as part of it. In reality, La Pergola & Bar Buca di Bacco is a separate restaurant that does not belong to the more well-known eatery, despite the similar name. After checking out the menu

177

at this more casual place, we like it and ask for a table for dinner. The wonderful ambience a few meters from the water with a fantastic view perpetuates real-life fantasy of another day in paradise.

I decide on the *spaghetti al pomodorino fresco e basilico* (spaghetti with cherry tomatoes and basil), and the friendly waiter nods as he approves my choice. After asking him to recommend a locally produced wine, he returns with a bottle of red wine, Costa d'Amalfi Tramonti Rosso from Tenuta San Francesco Winery. Toasting each other with glasses of this Italian wine, we enjoy repeating "Cin Cin," the Italian version of "Cheers."

While we wait for our meal, the sun disappears and twilight fills the sky. A beautiful bride and her groom stroll past us on the beach, while onlookers greet them with good wishes in Italian. "Auguri." They are holding glasses filled with what I assume is prosecco, while a wedding photographer waits nearby with his camera. Positano's reputation as one of the most popular locations for a destination wedding can be evidenced tonight.

After the lovely meal, we browse some of the busy beachfront shops and notice that the other restaurants are more crowded at this later hour. We decide to walk back before dark, and I must admit that without stopping for photos, the walk back to Hotel Pupetto really does take only ten minutes. Brava, Gabriella, for an accurate time estimate.

***

I almost cannot explain how mesmerizing this town is. You really have to experience it for yourself to fully understand its magnetic pull on my heart. I always want to keep coming back again and again to this slice of paradise on the Amalfi Coast.

Sorrento by Way of Pompeii

Since my brother and sister-in-law opt out of the excursion this last week in September of 2015, I'm traveling alone today. I arrive at the Salerno train station, courtesy of the shuttle bus from Hotel Olimpico, and I purchase a one-way ticket to Pompeii for today. I'm aware that once my train reaches Pompeii, I will then have to take the local Circumvesuviana to Sorrento. Weighing my transportation options earlier, I considered taking the ferry to Amalfi, and another ferry from there, but Giuseppe at the hotel desk recommends the train as a better option, so I follow his advice.

After standing on the platform for ten minutes waiting for my train, I discover from the updated sign above that it is delayed. When the delay time continues to be extended later and later, I decide to check whether another train to Pompeii might be scheduled anytime soon. To my pleasant surprise, I ascertain that one will depart in a little while, so I make my way to that platform and wait. After some time, I realize that I am at the wrong platform and scramble to get to the correct one. Luck is on my side, as I see the train is already on the track. Since this is a local train, no seats are assigned with the ticket, so I board and choose a seat, settling in for the ride. Moments later, a conductor enters the coach and informs all of the passengers that we now must move to yet another train. *Only in Italy*, I think, as I realize my good luck has just flown out the window.

At long last, more than an hour past the originally scheduled train departure time, I'm on my way to Pompeii. My plans today entail meeting Tina in Sorrento, so I call to inform her that I am running late because of the train delays. Prior to today, I have only met Tina virtually, through social media. She owns and operates the tour agency Discover Napoli Destinations and has made me an offer I couldn't refuse, promising to take me to a place in Sorrento known for a special type of biscotti that I can't find anywhere.

Once I arrive in Pompeii, I locate the *biglietto* window inside the train station to purchase my ticket for Sorrento. This day seems to be going from bad to worse, because now I'm told that I need to go to a different Pompeii train station, two kilometers down the road. Exasperated, I'm running short on patience. I can't believe my luck, or lack thereof. *Who would have thought that Pompeii has two train stations?* Rather than walk, I decide to take a taxi to the other train station. Several drivers are hanging around, so I assume all is good.

Wrong. My luck now escalates from bad to worse. When I approach a taxi driver to ask about a ride to the other station, he responds in English with this unwelcome news: "Oh, we have a big problem. No trains."

At first, I'm not sure he understands my inquiry. "What kind of problem?" I ask, grateful that at least he speaks English and we can understand each other.

"There is a train strike now, for four hours. No trains until five o'clock," he explains without a hint of emotion.

181

I can't believe this. What else can go wrong today? "What? Are you kidding me?"

He looks at me and answers without explanation. "No trains," he says, turning away from me and walking back toward the other drivers. They talk among themselves in Italian and smile as they look at me. I can imagine them having a good laugh at the American woman traveling alone and getting stuck in Pompeii because of a train strike. I'm not amused.

Strikes in Italy are commonplace, part of the lifestyle. They can occur with all modes of transportation—and they do, on a regular basis. Many times these limited-time *scioperi dei treni* (train strikes) are scheduled in advance, but sometimes they are unannounced. These limited work stoppages usually last from four to twenty-four hours and can be a real nuisance, like this one today.

I wonder why the ticket seller didn't mention it to me. Instead, he seemed happy to sell me a ticket. Thank God I have a cell phone, and I call Tina again to explain what's going on. She must hear the utter aggravation in my voice, because she stays calm and provides me with a solution.

She suggests I inquire about a bus to Sorrento. I thank her and let her know I'll be in touch once I'm on my way. I walk back inside the station to ask where I can catch a bus to Sorrento, and of course, I'm told there is no bus to Sorrento from here. This must be one of those situations that qualifies for "you can't get there from here." At this point I have strong doubts that I will ever make it to Sorrento before the day ends.

Frustrated now more than ever, I phone Tina again, this time to apologize and tell her I won't be able to meet her after all. To my utmost surprise, without pausing at all, she replies,

"All right. I am coming to get you. Just wait at the station, and I will be there in about forty minutes. I'll be driving a black car and wearing blue-and-white polka-dot pants."

Stunned, I cannot believe that a woman I don't even know is coming to my rescue with her car. She must be a saint. *Thank you, Tina.* It's almost too good to be true, but I'm hopeful once more.

Shortly after this, while I wait for Tina outside the station, another taxi driver approaches me. He speaks even better English than the first driver, and he informs me that there is no strike and that the other driver lied to me. He assures me that I can catch a train to Sorrento now, and he will be happy to give me a ride to the other train station. Do I believe this guy? Why would I? I have lost all confidence in taxi drivers and train station ticket sellers in Pompeii at this point. In my present mood, I don't care if I never see Pompeii again.

"It's too late now," I say in an irritated tone. "My friend is coming for me." He continues talking to me, and he even provides me with a map of Pompeii. I don't know if he is trying to redeem the reputation of taxi drivers or not, but I don't trust anyone here. A few minutes later, the original taxi driver returns, and he too informs me that the strike is over and the trains are running again. *What is wrong with this picture?*

Just before two o'clock, this heavenly angel named Tina arrives, true to her word. Overwhelmed and so grateful after all the chaos, I'm thrilled to see her and run toward her car. She smiles at me, and I open the passenger door and get inside as fast as I can. Relieved to leave this place of confusion, I can't stop talking, thanking her and reliving the past thirty minutes, sharing all the sordid details with her.

She is wonderful! The next part of this journey turns out to be the best part of the day!

***

Now that I am with a local Neapolitan, I foresee the rest of today as a fun time. With Tina at the wheel, I begin to unwind. I watch with awe as she maneuvers her car out of Pompeii and quickly locates the road to Sorrento. Adept at navigating Italian roads, she appears to think nothing of leaning her head out the window and yelling at another driver in Italian. I enjoy her aggressive attitude, and I have no doubt we'll get along great. I take an instant liking to this woman with short blonde hair, piercing blue eyes, and a magnetic smile, and we click immediately, conversing as though we've known each other for years. Unlike me, she is thin—like most Italians I've met. Maybe I should move to Italia to manage *la bella figura*!

As we ride toward Sorrento, it's as if I have my own personal tour guide. Tina points out all the noteworthy villas along the way and the towns we pass on the Sorrentine peninsula. Now I can say that I know the birthplace of Captain Francesco Schettino, who ran the Costa Concordia aground and would later be sentenced to sixteen years in jail. Tina explains that Castellammare di Stabia is well-known for a number of famous sailing men besides Schettino. Having lived here for such a long time, she is so knowledgeable about the area's history. Her passion for what she does is quite obvious, and she is a natural travel guide and more. Born in Naples to an American father and Italian mother, she describes herself as "half-and-half, Italo-American." She tells me she grew up in a totally bilingual and bicultural environment, attending American schools and spending a lot of time with her Italian friends.

Sharing so much more than what I might expect on an arranged tour, Tina offers to stop the car several times so I can admire the view and capture it with my camera. This drive along the coast is so awesome, one of the prettiest in Italy, and the weather is perfect today. The unpleasantness from the Pompeii train station is long forgotten on this wonderful, unplanned adventure.

We stop for lunch at Pizzeria da Franco and afterward for *dolci* at Bar Pollio (see Chapter 11). Now it's time for some serious shopping with a local. Life always seems better when I'm spending money with someone who knows how to negotiate the best deals. We stroll through Sorrento and make our way to the shopping area, where the streets become narrow alleys filled with vendors. Today my goal is to purchase a few more of those intarsia wooden music boxes. These are my favorite item from Sorrento, and I seem to remember a few shops on or near the famous shopping street of Via San Cesareo. "I know just where to go," Tina says with the authority of one who definitely is familiar with the area. "I think I remember a shop just around the corner."

Within minutes we arrive at one of these shops—not one where the artisans are working, but a beautiful store with a lovely selection of intarsia boxes. In no time I spot the music boxes I like and narrow my choice down to one style, which already has the exact music I want. Can you guess? The song is the classic, and one of my favorites, "Come Back to Sorrento." After seeing the price, I'm satisfied and pleased to have found what I need in such a short time and look forward to bringing these music boxes home. "These are just what I was hoping to find. I'll take three of them," I say to the saleswoman.

Before the sales clerk has a chance to reply, Tina speaks up in Italian. I catch the gist of what she is asking, but not the entire conversation. I'm not as fluent in the Italian language as I was two years ago, when I was in Italy for three months. The two women speak to each other, and then the saleswoman recalculates the price and hands me the sales invoice. As I look at it, Tina explains in English that she has just negotiated a discount for me, since I am purchasing three items. I thank the woman for her generosity, and she gives me a genuine smile. I see no indication that she is displeased to provide the discount.

"Grazie. Buona serata," she says as we leave the shop.

Outside the shop, Tina seems content with her deal-making and offers up a helpful explanation. "Always ask for a discount, especially when you are buying more than one item. It can't hurt, and they will almost always give you a better price. And you don't have to thank them for doing so. You deserve it."

Hmm. A new concept for me to ponder. Things are definitely different in Italy. I'm surprised, since this is not at all how retail sales work in the capitalistic economy of the States.

"Wow, really, Tina? I'd never think to ask for a discount. I thought the price was good."

"It is, but it can be better, so just remember this lesson whenever you go on your next shopping excursion."

Not only do I leave Sorrento with intarsia music boxes, but I learn a valuable travel tip today.

Now that I'm finished with my shopping agenda, Tina is on her own mission. "I want to stop for some *formaggio*," Tina tells me "This is the only place that makes the cheese the way I like it. My family will love it when I come home and surprise them with fresh mozzarella from Sorrento. Wait until you see this. *Andiamo.*" (Let's go.) After a short walk we arrive at her favorite cheese shop. Once inside, she greets the owner, who is on a first-name basis with her. Conversing in Italian, Tina introduces me as her American friend who is a travel blogger. I feel like a VIP.

I watch with great interest as the woman reshapes a huge amount of fresh mozzarella and creates a figure eight. Tina informs me that this is their signature. I'm amazed. It's beautiful and looks delicious.

After we leave the shop I keep track of the time, since I need to get to the SITA bus stop for my ride back to the Amalfi Coast. On our walk back to the car, Tina advises that I take the SITA bus to Amalfi, where I will pick up another bus for the remainder of the trip to Salerno, where I'm staying. We arrive at the parking spot, get inside her car, and we are on the way to the Circumvesuviana train station.

Fifteen minutes later, Tina announces that we are at the train station. "That's where you buy the bus ticket," she tells me, pointing toward a large umbrella in front of the station where two men are selling bus tickets. *Quite a sophisticated system*, I muse. It works, though, and for the incredibly low price of €7.60, I purchase a one-way bus ticket for the trip to Salerno.

I hug Tina goodbye and thank her for a wonderful day that I could never have hoped to plan on my own. She sends me back with a surprise souvenir, a calendar from Naples. I promise her that I'll return and let her show me the best of Naples. Until now, my fears of pickpockets and dangerous situations have kept me from visiting Napoli, but I'm enthusiastic to discover all that is good about her city. Ciao, my new friend, and grazie mille.

On the bus ride back, I once again marvel at this spectacular coastline, and I view it as if I'm experiencing it for the first time. Evening is approaching and the sunlight's reflections sparkle like diamonds dancing on the water. The sea's blue-green hues now take on a silvery appearance, and I'm captivated like a child on Christmas. No matter how often I am here, I never tire of the sheer splendor of the Amalfi Coast.

Hotel Pupetto 2016 Solo Writing

As a writer, I have learned from experience that discipline and time management are key to publishing a book. So many distractions easily get in the way of making time for writing. Phone calls, the internet, television, or procrastination all impact whether a writing goal is reached.

My first novel has been on the back burner for some time so I could write and publish *Colors of Naples and the Amalfi Coast*. But now, completing it becomes my new priority. And I know just the place to accomplish my writing goal and make this project a reality.

***

It's now September of 2016, and in less than a month I leave for Italy once again. This time is different, though, because my main purpose in going is to spend time in a beautiful, peaceful setting to chill out and to write. The Amalfi Coast — Positano, in particular — is that place where I feel most relaxed and inspired. For me, this special place on the Tyrrhenian Sea is magical and as close to paradise as I can imagine. When I am there I wish I could stay forever.

So this trip I am indulging my dreams and am staying in a beachside hotel, where I have a balcony that opens to the sea and I can hear the sound of the waves as they roll against the shore a few hundred feet away. Always able to find inspiration by the water, whether it's the Atlantic Ocean near my home in Florida or the Tyrrhenian Sea on the Amalfi Coast, I know I can complete the first draft of my manuscript on a beach in Positano.

This time, I am not going to Positano to play tourist. Instead, I am going to write, to be inspired to work on the novel that I began two years ago and hope to complete and publish in early 2017. While I am dedicating most of my time there to writing, I am not going to be a hermit and never leave the hotel. I plan on walking every day, and since staircases and uphill paths are the only way to reach the center of town, I'll be sure to get my daily dose of Italian exercise.

I plan to allow myself the luxury of doing a few things while there, but they are limited to only two excursions. I am intent on hiking the Path of the Gods, an activity that I never would have even considered a few years ago. I am in much better physical condition now, so I am eager to experience this walk high above the town. I hope to post photos on Facebook from that hike, even though I have no intentions of blogging while I'm in Positano to work on my book. After I return home, I will make time to blog about the experience.

Writers have their own preferences for writing. Some write early in the morning, some write at night, and most of the good ones write every day. It's all part of the writing process. I know I need silence when I write, and I like to be alone so I have no distractions. I like to write near the ocean, where the sounds of the waves drown out any other noises and distracting conversations. I find the water soothing. In the words of the poet E. E. Cummings, "For whatever we lose (like a you or a me) it's always ourselves we find in the sea." Being near the sea renews my spirit.

My dream to spend two weeks alone in a beautiful, relaxing place on the Amalfi Coast with the intent to write has come true. For years I've thought how inspiring it would be if I could spend a couple of weeks alone at the sea to write, to work on a book. And now I am making it happen.

I can't recall how many messages I've received from friends who either live in Italy or plan to be in Italy during the time I reserved to be there to write. Each of these friends is genuine in their expression of interest to meet up with me in Italy—for a glass of wine, a cup of cappuccino, for lunch. As much as I enjoy connecting with people and meeting with others who share my love for *bella Italia*, I know I need to remain true to my agenda and not make plans with others while I'm in Positano to write.

Quite a few well-known writers have been inspired by the beauty of Italy and have kept homes in or near Positano for many years. Gore Vidal had a sparkling white mansion in Ravello that could be seen jutting out high on the cliffs of the Amalfi Coast overlooking the azure Tyrrhenian Sea a thousand feet below. Some time ago it was listed for sale for $21 million. And I only recently found that Mick Jagger and Keith Richards of The Rolling Stones wrote "Midnight Rambler" while staying in a house in Positano for a few days on a holiday in 1969. Since I'm a big fan of The Stones, I find this story fascinating.

I'm beyond excited just thinking about staring at the shimmering sea and listening to the gentle sounds of the waves as I pen my first novel. With that visual in my mind, I arrange to stay at the same beachfront hotel where I spent five days last summer. Seven months ago, I emailed Hotel Pupetto and requested the same sea-view room with a balcony, and I was thrilled when Gabriella was able to reserve it for me at a special price. What more can I ask for?

I hope to find my inspiration on Fornillo Beach, so I can finish writing my current work in progress, my first novel, *Critical Cover-Up*.

***

It's the first of October, and I am here in Positano spending two weeks on the beautiful Amalfi Coast, soaking up the sun and working on *Critical Cover-Up*. I am so fortunate to fulfill a dream, which now is my reality. In this peaceful environment that I consider paradise, I discover my inspiration and my muse.

Hotel Pupetto, a small, family-run hotel on Fornillo Beach, is the ideal place for me to write. The stunning view of the sea from my hotel room balcony allows me to enjoy spectacular sunrises and sunsets. At night, I can sleep with the sliding door slightly ajar so I fall asleep to the soothing sounds of the quiet waves. In this special place I encounter a deep sense of tranquility. To be here alone provides me with the solitude I need to focus on writing, and I am happy.

My room is just as I remember — bright and clean, with a magnificent view of the sea. Tastefully decorated in soothing colors of seafoam-green and white, the ceramic tile floors complement the caramel-brown wicker chairs. The twin beds

I recall from my trip with Victoria last year are now pushed together to form a king-size bed, which is furnished with a light bedspread to match the rest of the room's décor.

"Am I really here? Alone? In Positano?" I have to pinch myself to believe it. I'm ecstatic and almost giddy. The door to my balcony is open a bit, as if to welcome me home, and I walk outside onto my personal terrace and sink down into one of the two reclining chairs. As I close my eyes for a minute, my thoughts transport me and time stands still. Everything is perfect. The sun warms my face and arms, and I stay in the moment. Life is good. Opening my eyes, I see the boats moored offshore and the bright violet bougainvillea blooming on a pergola beneath me. As I look around me, I notice the little touches I loved so much the first time. The folding, white, sling patio chairs are fitted with striped fabric that matches the room interior colors, and the patio floor is ceramic tile. I love the rectangular, wrought iron table with its ceramic-tiled tabletop in hues that balance the sling chair colors. Its design can only be the Amalfi Coast with its hand-painted scene of Positano. This veranda is one of my offices for the next two weeks, fulfilling a long-awaited fantasy.

After my indulgent daydream, I decide to get settled and unpack, so happy to have a place to call home where I won't be packing and unpacking every few days. I relish the thought of staying in one location for such an extended amount of time.

Since I'm not hungry for lunch yet, and the clouds look a bit threatening, I decide to walk into town to pick up a few supplies. I know I won't be eating in restaurants all the time during this trip, and since my room includes a mini refrigerator, I plan on making some quick meals for myself, so I'm thinking ahead.

I know the way into town by now and head straight toward The Wine Shop, my favorite of the two delis in Positano. I love the message inscribed on a sign displayed inside this shop: "Life is too short to drink bad wine." It is comprised of two rooms, one set up like a grocery and the other featuring a nice wine selection.

On the grocery side, fresh vegetables and fruits are available, as well as a complete meat and cheese counter. "Buona sera, Signorina," I say to the petite, smiling girl, barely tall enough for me to see her standing behind the meat case.

"Buona sera, what would you like?" she replies.

I order some salami and cheese, one hundred grams of each. She wraps them both up and hands me the package. After I pay for it in cash, I'm out the door and headed back to my haven on the beach before the rains start. October has more chance of rain than some other months, so I'm not too surprised. And I'm not disappointed about the weather, since I didn't come here to lay on the beach. I can write inside and under cover.

After my return to the hotel in a light drizzle, I relax a bit in my room before heading down the steps and into the terrace dining room of Ristorante Pupetto. Many of the tables are empty, since it's still early for dinner in Italy. Ciro, the handsome, pleasant manager, greets me and ushers me to a table. I order a glass of prosecco and some water while I peruse the menu.

Hungry for some light fare tonight, I begin with what Ciro describes as a specialty here, *fiori di zucca ripieni di ricotta con salsa di zucchini alla scapecce* (zucchini flowers stuffed with ricotta on zucchini cream). And catching a glimpse of the *pizzaiolo* stoking the wood fire in the brick-built oven, I opt for a margherita pizza. What else does one order on the Amalfi Coast, so close to Napoli, the birthplace of this pizza named for the Queen Margherita? The homemade bread sticks with just the right amount of fennel satisfy my appetite while I await my meal.

***

Well-rested after a full night of sleep in my new home away from home, I start to write in earnest today. After breakfast on the covered terrace, I retreat to my room, turn on my laptop, and begin to write the final chapters of *Critical Cover-Up*. In my estimation the book is approximately three-fourths complete, and I intend to complete the last part while I'm in Positano. In the quiet space of this room, I tune out everything and immerse myself in the characters of Allison, Paula, Detective Derning, and the others.

After an hour elapses, something seems to be amiss. Pushing myself away from the desk, I stand up, walk out onto my balcony, and stay in the moment, staring at the deep blue water. The sea is calm, the sun is shining, and a gentle breeze blows, sweeping the bougainvillea ever so slightly. Surrounded by nature in all her glory, I suddenly realize what's missing.

Rather than continuing to write in the privacy of my room, I go back inside, grab my computer, and move to the balcony, positioning myself in the comfortable lounge chair closest to the open sliding door. Here I'm able to make progress once again, as the thoughts flow, and I'm checking the words that appear on the screen as I type. Oblivious to whatever may be happening on the beach below me, I am inspired. Every once in a while I gaze out on the horizon, and as I observe the boats anchored offshore, I understand I am exactly where I need to be — where I want to be.

This sense of solitude fuels me. I like the idea that nobody knows what I am doing at this precise moment. No phone is ringing or vibrating, and no text messages are interrupting my train of thought. No Facebook or Twitter notifications are pinging. The freedom of unplugging so I can concentrate on my manuscript with the goal of completing the first draft in these two weeks energizes me in a way I have not experienced in the past.

I write for hours, until I'm hungry. Remembering that my refrigerator is stocked with fresh Parmesan cheese and hard salami already sliced, I prepare a light personal lunch to eat on my balcony. The ceramic table is the perfect size for my afternoon *pranzo*. A bottle of *acqua naturale* and the cheese and meat charcuterie hits the spot, especially since I plan to have dinner later at the restaurant.

My days continue like this, writing on my veranda and then taking a walk into town to look around, shoot photos, and also for exercise. I am walking an average of three miles a day, and the hills and stairs don't bother me anymore. Sometimes I head into town just for the exercise, with no other intentions at all. I break it up and walk to places I've not been in the past, and I'm discovering new staircases that serve as shortcuts to reach the higher streets near the La Sponda bus stop.

Meals at Hotel Pupetto are discounted by ten percent for all guests, so that is a nice perk when dining there. On rainy days, the idea of staying in and eating at Ristorante Pupetto are even more appealing. And the rain makes it easier to stay in and write, rather than being tempted to sightsee.

On the far end of the terrace, closer to town, few people occupy the chairs and tables, as the area is not covered by a roof, only a pergola with grapevines and lemons. Though unprotected, it's beautiful just the same, with an inspiring view of the serene water. Some days, in the early afternoon, I switch out my writing location from my balcony to this open terrace. I bring my laptop, my phone, and a bottle of water with me and set up my "desk." I am far enough away from other guests so as not to be distracted, and I am able to work undisturbed. Usually one of the waiters asks if I'd like something to drink or to eat, since lunch is served throughout the afternoon, but I opt to wait until later for a meal.

Euphoric to find myself in this seafront location I have envisioned in dreams, I find my inspiration and write for hours. Occasionally, I look out to the sea and imagine what my character is going to do next, asking myself questions. *How will Allison get herself out of this situation and still save face?* As I write, the story is progressing, but I don't yet have that turning point, the one that will make a difference in the plotline.

As I sit outside and let my thoughts pull me deeper into the story, I finally have it. All of a sudden, I have an epiphany, and the entire story propels forward, triggering the action in a surprising direction, and I feel the excitement. I can hardly believe it, but I know that being here at this beach on the Amalfi Coast is the source of that inspiration. I am elated!

I've been writing nonstop for almost two hours, but I continue to type, advancing the story of my characters, and I like where it is going. I am sold on it. I know that if I don't find the story thrilling, I can't expect my readers to like it. But now I have a reason to believe that my novel's twists and turns will excite the readers enough that they will want to keep reading and won't see what's coming next. Writing fiction is much more difficult for me, having written three nonfiction books prior to this. My *eureka!* moment, my striking realization today on the terrace of Hotel Pupetto, is a huge move forward, and I definitely need to celebrate later with some prosecco. I think I'll head up to Ristorante Mediterraneo tonight (see Chapter 5).

***

As I write, I sometimes find it necessary to access the internet to research some things. Since the quality of the Wi-Fi is sketchy, I become frustrated, and decide to mention this to Ciro. To my surprise, he provides me with some free advice, which turns out to be a huge advantage. "Yes, I know our Wi-Fi isn't so good, because we are on some kind of sharing plan. So here is what you do. Go next door to the little beach bar. You know the bar, Da Ferdinando?"

"No, I haven't been there."

"No? You must go. Just walk over there and order a coffee for one or two euros. Then ask them for the Wi-Fi password. They use the same one for three or four days in a row, and you can get online over there. I think maybe it even works from your room, and it's stronger than ours."

Wow, I'm thinking to myself. It's amazing that the hotel manager shares this secret with me. But this is Italy and they play by different rules. Later, after I'm done writing for the afternoon, I wander over there. It's not crowded at the moment and, true to Ciro's word, an espresso costs one euro. When I inquire about Wi-Fi, a friendly young man who works here provides me with the password. This place is great, right on the beach but under cover, so bad weather is not a problem. A laid-back vibe defines this beach bar that serves breakfast and lunch, as well as coffee, beer, vino, and cocktails. Chica, the cute, white, friendly poodle is part of the Ferdinando family too, so this place is pet-friendly. I get the sense that a lot of the people know each other, and the atmosphere is like a family. I like it very much.

I return here almost every afternoon with my laptop and do some writing, but they close at five o'clock, so my time is limited. Once in a while, I use the Wi-Fi to make a WhatsApp call, and I can't complain about the connection quality because it's good most days. With the six-hour time difference between here and the States, I can call my boyfriend and enjoy a conversation, so everything here is a win-win.

I've switched to ordering Caffè Americano instead of espresso every afternoon now, and after just one day, the waiters remember my preference. "Caffè Americano?" they ask, handing me the Wi-Fi password as I take my seat. At first the password stayed the same for several days, but now they are changing it daily. And their internet access does work from my hotel room, mostly from the balcony rather than the room. But when they close for the day, the Wi-Fi is also off, so no access exists in the evenings.

I pay €1.80 for my Americano coffee. I can't find a better deal. This family-run Da Ferdinando Beach Bar has been a fixture here on Fornillo Beach since 1951 and is owned by Guido, who is always so pleasant and friendly. His son Ferdinando and nephew Andrea work here, and I think the others are all part of the family in one way or another. They make me feel like I'm part of their family too.

Between my little family here and the one I've come to know at Hotel Pupetto, I experience a real sense of belonging during these two weeks in Positano. Hotel Pupetto is my true home away from home, and I love it here. Veronica, Gabriella, and Gabriella's mother, Lucia, share stories with me about their families, and I even meet Gabriella's little girl, Alicia. All the waiters—Fabio, Antonino, Domenico, Raffaele, and Francesco—know my favorite foods and beverages and go out of their way to make me feel special every day. Even Giuseppe, the chef, and the housekeepers, Anna and Laetizia, greet me with smiles and a warm *buongiorno* and *come sta*, so I can practice my Italian with them.

The season is coming to an end here on this coast, and as I look down toward Spiaggia Grande, with its hundreds of orange beach umbrellas and chairs lined up in rows, only a few sun worshippers are around. I wonder what this place is like during the winter. Gabriella tells me that by mid-October everything on the beach closes down, and the employees go home until the spring. I get the idea that after working seven days a week for the entire season, these employees appreciate the time off. And I'm told that Italy has a program similar to unemployment in the States. For an employee to qualify, he or she must work a minimum amount of time in a given year; I think it may be six months. After that, the government subsidizes workers a specific amount of money during the months they are not working. This arrangement plays a significant role in the yearly income for workers in the hospitality industry, which often is seasonal.

***

I'm going to miss Positano and the people I've come to know. Part of my heart will be here forever, and I know I'm coming back as soon as I can. After I return home I'll be busy with the rewriting process. My manuscript will soon be in the hands of four beta readers, whose feedback will be invaluable to me. I'll review their comments and continue with the rewriting process and the third draft. After that I will hand it over to my editor, who will send it back to me to make more changes and start the fourth draft.

A good editor and award-winning author once told me to expect to write at least five drafts before publishing a book. When I first heard this I thought she was crazy, but I have since learned that she was right. I'll then be working on my cover, collaborating with an expert I know and trust. I plan to release my novel as an e-book as well as a paperback edition, and it will be available on Amazon.com as well as in the UK and other countries. If all goes well, I am hoping for a spring release date, but in reality, I think it may take longer. *Vediamo.*

Love on the Amalfi Coast

Today is Friday, May 4, 2018, and I'm returning to the Amalfi Coast, but this time everything is different. I'm traveling with someone special, someone who's made a difference in my life for the last three years. While I never expected to meet someone and fall in love again, I've learned that life is full of surprises. And now I'm sharing my passion for Italy with Richard Allen, the man I love. This is his first trip to Italy, and he's already fallen in love with it. What could be better?

After spending the past six days in Rome, Richard and I are on our way to Naples. Exactly on time, our high-speed Italo train arrives at 10:20 a.m. at Napoli Centrale station. Francesco, from Drive Amalfi, is waiting for us on the train platform, holding a yellow sign with my name on it. He will be driving us to Positano, which will be our home for the next five nights. After greeting each other, we walk through the station together, past all the designer shops, and I can't help but notice it's quite a bit more modern than I remember. Francesco confirms that the station has recently been updated and is much safer now, with state-of-the-art security. Good to know. Twenty minutes later, Richard and I are in the back seat of his Mercedes car, and he pulls away in a light drizzle.

Francesco is a true gentleman, friendly, charming, and polite. He's also professional, dressed in a navy-blue sports jacket, dress slacks, and a tie. As he drives away from the airport area, he points out a red traffic stoplight in the shape of a heart. "Look at this. It's the only one in Naples," he says.

I've never seen this before. "Wow, that is so cool. Very romantic," I reply.

I allow my mind to wander. Perhaps this is the harbinger of an amorous vacation in my favorite Italy destination. I'm excited that we're on our way. Unfortunately it's raining, but we didn't come here for the weather.

After a while the rain subsides, but the sky remains overcast. As we're driving, Francesco points out Vesuvius, shrouded in dense cloud cover. We pass Pompeii and can just catch a glimpse of the ancient ruins out the left car window. Soon we pass Sorrento and the island of Capri. As we continue, Francesco points out the town of Gragnano and explains that it is the most famous place in the world for pasta production. We drive through the little towns of Meta and Piano di Sorrento, and while these places ring familiar to me, I'm aware that Richard is seeing them for the first time.

Soon the cloud cover breaks and the sun appears. As we get closer to our destination, I can see a town in the distance. Francesco informs us that we are looking at Praiano, which is actually past Positano, but from this vantage point it appears to be the closer location. As we approach Positano, traffic grinds to a halt, and the road is now completely blocked. Vehicles appear to be moving in only one direction.

"We are going to be here for a while," Francesco informs us. "I have seen this happen before. I will notify the hotel that we will arrive later than planned."

Francesco calls Hotel Pupetto and explains the situation in Italian. He tells us that the receptionist has already heard about the blockage from another driver, and she is not surprised to learn that we might arrive later than originally scheduled. Once the traffic begins to flow again, Francesco drives us as far as he can, to the parking garage area, and unloads our bags for the porters, who are waiting to transport them to the hotel. Now we have to travel on foot the rest of the way. Richard is a good sport as we walk all the way down the hundreds of steps that I had described to him before this trip. We are fortunate to be able to stop at Hotel Victoria and take the elevator down four flights, saving some steps.

By the time we reach Hotel Pupetto, it's close to one o'clock. Gabriella and Veronica are there to greet us with smiles, and the reception seems like old home week. Hugs and kisses and introductions are made, we check in, and Veronica ushers us up the stairs to our room.

We get settled into Room 221, although it's not the room I expected. This isn't the same room I had on my last visit. Instead, it's the room next door, a more spacious room with an extra bed. What a nice surprise to receive an upgrade. The spectacular view from the balcony is the same as I remember—just beautiful. I like that it's not exactly the same room, because now that I'm here with Richard, this time is even more special. He likes the room very much and is blown away by the view. "I'm so happy, baby," he says. "We are finally here. Now I can see what you've been talking about all this time." I'm thrilled that my dream is now a reality, and everything seems wonderful.

After we relax for a while, enjoying having no agenda and just being here together, we decide to go downstairs for some lunch. I immediately recognize Domenico, the headwaiter, and I introduce Richard to him. After we are seated we order a beverage. I have a prosecco, and Richard has a glass of red wine. A caprese salad, warm pumpkin soup, and zucchini flowers sound good too, and afterward, Domenico brings us a complimentary limoncello.

With the help of Gabriella and Veronica, we are successful in establishing Wi-Fi connections on our phones, and I'm happy to discover that the signal is much stronger than last time. Once we return to our room, we realize that the Wi-Fi works well, and I'm glad not to have the frustration with it that I experienced when I was here eighteen months ago. Even though I'm not working on this trip, Richard and I both like to stay connected, so the improved internet is a plus. With a little help from Nadia, a new receptionist, we learn how to turn on the heat, since Positano is cooler than expected today.

After unwinding a little more from our travels, we decide not to leave the hotel, but to eat dinner here this evening since it's rainy and we're somewhat tired. Clear vinyl window shades are in place, making the enclosed terrace a comfortable temperature. Richard orders a cabernet for both of us and then chooses a grilled leg of lamb for his entrée. I'm dying for pizza margherita, now that I'm on the Amalfi Coast, so I place my order, and we choose *insalata mista* to share. Dinner on the restaurant terrace as we overlook the Tyrhennian Sea can't be any more romantic. It's perfect being here together.

Tonight, the other headwaiter, Francesco, is here. His smile reveals that he remembers me, and I introduce him to

Richard. I also recognize Giuseppe, the *pizzaiolo*, and Raffaele, one of the young waiters. I'm so happy here, and it's like a dream come true. Richard seems really happy too.

***

Back in our room, we leave our sliding glass door to the balcony closed for the night, since the outside air is cool and the heat is on, but we can still hear the pounding of the waves. They're louder than I remember, thanks to the storms the area has been experiencing. No ferry boats operated today or yesterday, we were told, due to the bad weather. Always optimistic though, both Veronica and Gabriella promised that tomorrow should be better. Tonight we fall asleep listening to the rhythmic sound of the waves.

Sunlight filters through the curtain and wakes us at six o'clock the next morning. Not ready to begin our day so early, we pull the covers over our heads and go back to sleep. I had no idea the sun rose so early here! We finally wake up around eight o'clock but we don't go down to breakfast until nine thirty. With no need to get up early and no plans to do anything, this is the life of leisure for sure, and I'm loving every minute of it. The sensation of not having to do anything and not having to be responsible to post anything on social media is just such a freeing feeling for me.

The self-serve breakfast buffet is delicious, and the atmosphere on the terrace is an added bonus. Raffaele brings me a cup of cappuccino and a cup of tea for Richard. Before we go back up to the room I present Gabriella with a gift I brought for her seven-month-old baby boy, Michele. With true excitement, she opens the package and holds up the little blue sailor outfit. I can tell she is thrilled, and that makes me smile. Michele is a real cutie pie with the bluest eyes I have ever seen. I also give her and Veronica their autographed copies of *Critical Cover-Up*, the book I finished writing when I was here in 2016, and have another book, *Colors of Naples and the Amalfi Coast*, for Gabriella, since she gave her copy to the hotel. I feel like I'm back with my family here, and Richard is soaking it all in and loving every minute of it too.

Upstairs in our room we take it easy, resting and catching up on some news on one of the few English television channels until one o'clock. Out on the balcony I take a few pictures as the bright sun appears to sparkle and dance on the water. The outside temperature feels mild, in the mid-60s, according to the weather app, and I feel comfortable without a jacket. I remember that here on the coast, the temperatures dip in the morning and the evening, and then after eleven or so the air becomes much warmer.

Since we're going into town, I dress in sandals and capris, and Richard wears his new blue leather jacket he bought in Florence. He's a trooper, walking up all the inclines and stairs on the way to the center of town. Once we reach the trendy restaurants on the beach, like Chez Black, Buco di Bacco, and l'Incantro, the path is flat. Along the beachfront, we see the locals setting up the summer concessions at Spiaggia Grande. It's a little late in the season, but they've had such bad weather that they haven't had a chance to get everything ready yet.

Some people are on the beach and in the water, despite the cooler weather. We don't get very far past the stairs when Richard says, "Let's have lunch first," so we head back down the steps. He chooses Buco di Bacco, and I feel so special. Of course, I'm reminiscing about the scene in the movie *Under the Tuscan Sun*, and I'm lucky to have a man who takes charge and is so romantic. He looks at me and says, "Hey, we're in Positano. We have to eat here."

He walks inside the restaurant and asks for a table by the window. Wouldn't you know they have the perfect table with the best view of the sea from the open window. We are seated and meet Pasquale, our waiter. Richard suggests wine and chooses a Merlot for both of us. Pasquale obliges us by taking our picture by the window, and then we order. We decide on an appetizer of grilled octopus with artichokes, burrata cheese, and balsamic vinegar. I choose ravioli stuffed with burrata cheese in yellow cherry tomato sauce and eggplant. Richard orders the fried *baccalà* on cream of chickpea and cricket red peppers. We also have *acqua naturale*. The meal is fantastic.

We can't help but notice the two people seated at the table next to us. They are speaking English and obviously are Americans. Their food choices leave something to be desired, as the man orders spaghetti and meatballs, and the lady orders a plain chicken breast, which isn't on the menu. Richard and I cannot imagine how anyone can come to Italy and not totally embrace the culture and the lifestyle, especially in an elite place like this restaurant. We are so much on the same page, and it means everything to me that he is enjoying each moment in Italy as much as I am. I don't think I could love this man any more than I do now.

After our satisfying and tasty lunch, we walk up the hill to Via Cristoforo Colombo, taking a few breaks along the inclined route, and again, no complaining from Richard. Once more, I am impressed by how well he is navigating all the steps. I have to give him a lot of credit for his positive attitude and effort on his first time in Positano.

I'm searching for a ceramic shop, because I'd like to buy a replacement ceramic olive oil container for my son Brian. The first store doesn't have what I'm looking for, but we soon come across a second shop, where I find the perfect vase and purchase it. The kind manager carefully wraps it in Bubble Wrap, as if he knows I need to travel with this. I love the Italians.

After that we turn around and go back down the hill to La Zagara, a famous *pasticceria* which we spotted on our way up here. Earlier, I had suggested stopping in here for a coffee and a dessert. When we arrive, we walk inside and are told we can sit outside in the garden. Our table is lovely in this covered, outdoor paradise surrounded by fragrant orange trees. The romantic, intimate setting is perfect for couples in love like us. Since we are not in any hurry, we take time to embrace the experience, and after a while a waiter appears to take our order. I order a cappuccino, and Richard orders a coffee with ginseng. Then we order a Sicilian cannolo, my first since arriving in Italy. We also decide to try the tempting *torta alle mandorle e limone*, something I've never tasted, but I have heard that it's a specialty pastry from this region. The flavor in the cake is so distinct. "I'd love to find the recipe for this almond cake and try to make it at home," I say to Richard. He smiles at me and voices his approval. I'm happy he likes the idea. Both of these desserts are delicious. I take a few pictures in the outside garden here, where the view is delightful. I can see the dome of the cathedral from the back corner of the terrace. I notice the colorful ceramic floor tiles with blue and yellow designs. This place has been in existence for almost seventy years and is one of the oldest *pasticcerias* in Positano. Anyone who has been to Positano, including many celebrities, has heard of La Zagara.

It's already four thirty, and we're supposed to have some rain this evening, so we decide to head back. We stop to take a few pictures along Via Positanesi d'Americana, the pedestrian passageway back to Fornillo Beach and our hotel. We take a few selfies, and I'm glad I'm wearing my black hat today. I feel like a movie star.

***

Awakening to a sky that is blue in the west and a gray cloud settling in over the higher parts of Positano, I see the sun peeking out every now and then. The sea is calm on this Sunday, the ferries are running, and the temperature is mild. Small powerboats transport a few passengers to and from shore, and at least twenty boats are anchored offshore. A handful of people stroll along the quiet, stony beach at a leisurely pace

Next door, Da Ferdinando Beach Bar is not yet open, but I hear a lot of pounding and banging and can see that the workers have made much progress in the concession construction since yesterday. With some luck, it might open in the next day or two, so we can enjoy a cappuccino there before we leave.

"Maybe today we should take the ferry to Amalfi," Richard proposes. I agree, since the temperature is in the sixties with no rain in the forecast, and the weather for the remainder of our time here suggests a fifty percent chance of rain every day. Since this trip is about the two of us as a couple, I want to make sure Richard feels comfortable and isn't doing things just to please me, so I like that he makes the suggestion. We always share our thoughts, and I realize that yesterday's uphill trek to Via Cristoforo Colombo and back down definitely challenged him. Just a little over three months post-knee replacement surgery, he's managing this terrain better than most travelers might, but the three hundred-plus steps down to our hotel have a cumulative effect and take a toll on the body.

I'm more than happy that he recommends taking the boat to Amalfi today, because the ride will allow him to experience the view of the Amalfi coast from the vantage point of the sea for the first time. I know what that's like, and I'm eager for him to encounter it too, since that's an entirely different experience than seeing it from a bus or in a car. I know we won't have to do extensive walking in Amalfi, since we'll be content to stay in the center, where the cathedral and fountain dominate the main piazza. We can enjoy a leisurely lunch there and do a bit of shopping. Why add stress when it's not necessary? *Il dolce far niente.*

After a leisurely breakfast on the terrace, Richard and I check times for the ferry to Amalfi. Gabriella informs us that the next boat leaves at 10:00 a.m., and the one after is scheduled to depart at 11:10 a.m. To insure we're not totally stressed trying to catch the earliest ferry, we opt for the later departure and return to our room for a bit.

At the dock, when we purchase the tickets for the 11:10 a.m. ferry, for the reasonable price of €8.00 per person each way. We are told the scheduled departure will be at 11:20 a.m. instead. *Va bene.* (It's okay.) We are in Italy and are in no hurry.

"Let's sit on the top, if it's okay with you," I suggest, "so we can have a good view. We should try to find a seat on the left side of the boat." Richard is fine with that, and as soon as the ferry leaves, I regret not wearing a jacket, because the

211

wind is strong and I'm freezing cold. I'm thankful the ride isn't that long.

But we have a great view of the shoreline, and Richard is impressed upon seeing the coast from the water. His reaction pleases me immensely, and I love the fact that he's enjoying this with me.

On the twenty-minute ride to Amalfi, I recognize Praiano and Furore and see the old convent, which is now a hotel, high above Amalfi. As we pull closer to Amalfi, an Azmara cruise ship is conspicuously docked offshore.

Soon we disembark, and upon entering the town I point out to Richard the hotel where I stayed when I traveled here alone four years ago. After admiring the Cathedral of Saint Andrew and the fountain with the same name, we browse around the center. The sun is shining here, and it's a perfect day for walking around Amalfitown, as the locals refer to this city. We walk inside Pasticceria Andrea Pansa, which opened in 1830, and the aroma of chocolate and sweets more than satisfies our cravings. Good thing we're not hungry. We check out the ceramic shops, a leather shop, and L'Arco Antico, a paper shop, where I buy some authentic Amatruda note cards and Richard purchases a beautiful pen. We find a supermarket, where I buy some *torrone di limone* and a small box of laundry soap to wash some clothes by hand when we return to our hotel.

Both of us enjoy shopping, so we stop in at a few clothing shops too. Not that we need them, but we can't resist some cool Italian sunglasses, and I also find a white linen blouse at a clothing shop called il Buco. After trying it on, Maria helps me decide that I like it enough to take it home with me. It's a fun day, and while the narrow street is busy with other shoppers, it isn't packed. That cruise ship we noticed earlier is a mid-size vessel, carrying only seven hundred passengers, so the town isn't inundated with cruise day-trippers.

Near the end of the street and away from the busier area of Amalfi, an inviting outdoor restaurant in Piazza Santo Spirito attracts Richard's attention. "Are you hungry for lunch? What do you think of this place?" he asks.

I love the look of this trattoria, with its overhead canopies and white tablecloths. I glance at the menu and see a great selection. "Looks like the perfect place for lunch. I like that it's a little bit out of the way," I reply.

Richard notices a table for two right next to the street, where we can easily people-watch. We sit down at this table at La Taverna del Duca, and the atmosphere is exactly what we hoped to find today. Next to an eighteenth-century stone fountain built into a wall and intertwined with an elaborate nativity scene *presepe*, this alluring ristorante is also the perfect location to relax while we dine on seafood and pasta. The marinated anchovies are especially tasty, as is the *scamponi alla griglia in umido* (scampi with large prawns), and the penne *arrabbiata* is enhanced with a generous amount of sautéed cherry tomatoes. An entertaining group of four musicians regale us with their renditions of "Volare" and "Tu Vuò Fà L'Americano" to make this a wonderful experience in Amalfi.

On the walk back toward the entrance to town, we stop at a gelato shop next to Saint Andrew's Cathedral, where some vacant tables are available outside. The gelato is homemade, and they offer thirty-six flavors, including, of course, limoncello. I choose *amarena* and pistachio, and Richard orders *stracciatella* and mint. Not a bad price at only €9.50 for both. The people who work here are very nice and are also happy to allow us to use the bathrooms upstairs.

Richard and I sit outside and watch everyone as they go by, counting our blessings for the simple pleasures of life. After some time, we decide to take the 3:00 p.m. boat back to Positano. We spend the rest of the day in our room until we walk downstairs for dinner at 8:00 p.m.

"I love the feeling of doing nothing," I say.

Richard smiles and hugs me. "Me too."

***

It's Monday and we decide to spend a romantic day in our room enjoying each other's company. Tonight we plan to go to Ristorante Mediterraneo for dinner and to see Pietro Rainone sing. To reach this restaurant, which is located in the upper area of Positano on Viale Pasitea, requires a lot of walking up steep steps. Rain is in the forecast for tonight, so we decide to leave around seven o'clock to get ahead of it.

"I know you really don't want to go, do you?" I say as our departure time draws near.

With a look that defies excitement, he replies, "Well, it's just . . ."

He doesn't need to finish the sentence. I can tell he would rather not go. I know his legs hurt, and he isn't thrilled with the prospect of walking up more steps.

I really want to go, and I convince myself that once we get there, he will enjoy it. So, even knowing we have several hundred steps to climb each way, we head out.

We leave Hotel Pupello through the restaurant and head out the side door to start the climb up the steps. From here to Hotel Victoria there are at least one hundred very steep and uneven stone steps. When we reach Hotel Victoria, we are to take an elevator and then walk along a road and climb some more steps until we arrive at the street where Mediterraneo is located.

As we are climbing the first hundred steps, I can see that Richard is not fond of the exercise. I don't say anything, and we keep trudging along. Every time we reach a landing and turn the corner, another long set of stairs greets us. For some reason, the climb seems longer, with more turns and steps than I recalled it to be. At one point, I say, "The elevator is right here," believing that it is just around the next corner. Richard climbs the steps about ten feet behind me, and when I turn the corner, my stomach knots up. There is no elevator here. Now I am forced to give him the bad news, and naturally, he is not happy. At least forty more stairs await us. I regret saying anything that suggested we were almost at the elevator.

When we finally reach the silver-colored outside elevator, I push the button and nothing happens. I push the Reception button and explain that we're waiting to take the elevator up to Hotel Victoria. The male voice replies, "Elevator not working. You must take the steps."

At this point I am frustrated, and I assume Richard is completely upset. We have no option except to keep walking. Resigned, we continue along the walkway until we eventually reach Hotel Victoria.

We enter and see a green elevator, and now I recall that the reception area is upstairs. Since the male voice directed us to take the stairs, I assume this elevator is not functioning, so we begin climbing what seems to be six flights of steps inside the hotel to the top floor where the main desk is located. I am sure Richard is cursing under his breath, because I certainly am. This is way more steps that I had anticipated. Both of us are compelled to continue, since we are already committed to the challenge. Poor Richard is sweating and the overexertion is etched on his face. I feel terrible. The last thing I want is to add additional stress, and it seems that is exactly what I'm doing. When we finally reach the reception desk, I take a moment to catch my breath and inquire about the elevator, now that I am face-to-face with the male receptionist.

"Buona sera, Signore. If the elevator is broken, I wish someone could have told the receptionist at Hotel Pupetto."

The man looks at me with a blank stare and replies, "The elevator is working inside the hotel."

I look at him incredulously and ask, "What? You told me the elevator didn't work."

"The old elevator to Pupetto doesn't work. It never works."

Now I'm confused and feel like a real fool. Obviously I didn't remember this detail from my earlier trip here, forcing us to walk up six more flights of steps than we needed to. I feel especially bad for Richard, since he is the one overdoing it with his new knee. If a hole in the floor could open up right here, I'd love to fall into it and disappear.

In silence, Richard and I walk back outside and spot the church that Gabriella had mentioned when she gave me directions. Per her instructions, we find another staircase just to the right of it, which consists of approximately forty or fifty more steps, and we head up toward our destination. At the top of the staircase, we finally arrive on a street, and yes, it is Viale Pasitea, where the restaurant is located. We turn right onto this one-way street, and I get excited because I think I see the restaurant, but as we inch closer, sweaty and tired, I realize it's not what I thought. We need to walk a bit farther, and I cringe as I have to give Richard this disappointing news. I am convinced he's ready to kill me and certain that he regrets the entire idea of coming here this evening. I stay hopeful, though, that once inside, he can relax and we can salvage what I had hoped would be a wonderful evening.

When we get to the restaurant, we are seated in the covered terrace by the gregarious host, Rodrigo. But as soon as we sit down, Richard notices a huge warming light beaming down on him. This is the last thing he needs after the strenuous trip to get here. "This isn't going to work. I'm going to see if we can sit inside, where hopefully it will be cooler," he says, and disappears to find Rodrigo.

Pietro, the musician, arrives and recognizes me. He stops by my table to say hello while Richard is inside talking with Rodrigo. Because of the tension I sense between Richard and me, I don't say too much. Richard is exhausted and somewhat irritated. I feel bad about the whole situation. This is not the kind of experience I had hoped tonight would be.

Soon Richard reappears and motions for me to follow him inside. Thankfully, the smiling Rodrigo seats us at an inside table just across from the open kitchen. Perfect. I thank Rodrigo for being so accommodating. He even provides a napkin for Richard to use to wipe his face. We order drinks — a prosecco for me and a glass of red wine for Richard. I suggest an appetizer, and we decide on prosciutto with melon and some bruschetta. Things seem to settle a bit. Pietro comes by and sings, and I am a bit subdued, thinking this is not a time for too many words.

By the time we are halfway through our appetizers, we talk about the less-than-pleasant challenge of getting here. Richard confides in me that his hesitancy this evening was a bit more than just anticipation of all the steps we'd have to climb. Apparently, the romantic afternoon in our hotel room had taken a bit of a toll on him. After all, we're not teenagers anymore.

I smile, grateful that he has shared his feelings with me. "Maybe we should have left a little later," I say.

"I should have said something before we left," Richard says.

Talking things over is always better, and the tension begins to melt away.

"You know, I noticed a taxi on the street when we arrived here. Maybe when we leave we can take a taxi to the center of town and walk back the other way, where there aren't the type of steep steps we encountered coming here," I suggest. Richard doesn't comment.

We order our dinner and Pietro is back, serenading us with his mandolin and, later, his guitar. The atmosphere slowly becomes more enjoyable, a little more like what I had anticipated. Richard seems to like Pietro's performance, saying, "He's really pretty good. Better than I expected." I'm happy to see a smile from Richard, despite the rocky start to the evening.

The chefs in the kitchen complement the musical entertainment, singing along with the gregarious, fun-loving Pietro from time to time. The waiters chime in too. This is one big happy family here. Our meal arrives and is tasty. I ordered eggplant parmesan, and he ordered a beef scallopini in sauce. As more of the diners start singing along, we join in too and even engage in a long conversation after dinner with a couple sitting near us. Pete and Karen, from the Durham area of North Carolina, are an interesting couple who tell us a story about how they decided on the spur of the moment to come to Italy. Richard enjoys the camaraderie, and by the end of the evening he is even requesting songs in Italian and laughing. We stay for three hours and end up having a great evening.

What I love is how Richard turns the night around by taking charge and finding another way to go back to the hotel. "I know how to go back. Three staircases past the restaurant will be an easier way. There will be a lot of steps, but they won't be as steep. And we will end up in the center of town. From there we can walk back the way we know to our hotel."

After the complimentary, obligatory limoncello, we pay the bill and say our goodbyes. By now it's dark and raining, but we have umbrellas, and Richard walks confidently down the street beside me toward the third staircase. I like how these staircases are named as if they are roads, like Salita Lepanto.

"How did you know the way to get back?" I ask.

Richard smiles at me and says, "I asked a waiter." My heart is light and I'm happy. I don't mind walking home in the rain together. Even though there are about four hundred steps down, maybe more than coming up, they are wider, more level, and nowhere near as steep as those we traversed earlier this evening. Some of the staircases are not well-lit. Like a gallant knight, Richard precedes me as we walk, cautioning me as we approach wider, steeper steps. This trip back to the hotel is actually fun, and Richard even tells me he likes it. So, something good comes from something bad tonight, and we both smile and laugh all the way back. I promise him that tomorrow we don't have to do anything unless he wants to. I am fine with doing nothing and staying at the hotel all day. I love this man.

***

219

This morning at breakfast I splurge and order Nutella pancakes from the menu, a first for me. I have to admit, I now understand the attraction of this creamy hazelnut and cocoa spread. These pancakes are to die for, and thank you, Raffaele, for the delicious cappuccino. Today looks like a rainy day, so Richard and I spend the rest of the morning in our room.

At one o'clock, I'm surprised when he suggests we walk into town, since the sky is clear and his legs have recuperated from last night. The ten-minute walk seems easy to both of us by now, and once there, we cruise the shops a bit and stroll around the beach area. After a few minutes, the sight of the beach restaurants convinces Richard he is hungry, and he suggests lunch at Le Tre Sorelle, a restaurant started sixty-five years ago by three sisters. I love the ambience here on the beach. It's a great place for people-watching. We have a table for two, where we both face the water. The choice is ideal.

After that high-carb breakfast, I order a rocket salad with cherry tomatoes and Parmesan cheese, and grilled vegetables. Richard orders chicken with porcini mushrooms in a lemon sauce, and we share the salad. Every bite tastes delicious, and we savor the time, knowing full well that a waiter in Italy will never bring the check or ask us to leave until we signal that we're ready. By three-thirty, we are back in our room on this now cloudy, overcast afternoon. The rain never comes, and I'm beginning to think that it hovers over the mountains and never makes it to sea level. It's of no consequence though, since today is our last day in Positano and relaxation is our only goal.

For our last dinner in Positano, we decide to eat at Ristorante Pupetto and find our special table that Domenico always reserves for us in the corner of the restaurant. Richard looks forward to *branzino* (sea bass) tonight. I'm having rigatoni *pomodoro* and a margherita pizza made by Giuseppe. We might as well enjoy our last dinner on the Amalfi Coast. Staying here with Richard is all I had hoped it would be and more. I'm very happy.

Tomorrow, our driver from Drive Amalfi is scheduled to pick us up in the late morning, and we fly to Catania as we head to Taormina for the remaining five days of what has, so far, been a beautiful trip together.

***

In anticipation of our early departure for Sicily today, I packed last night, and we are at breakfast by eight o'clock this morning. The porter picks up our bags by nine so he can transport them to the parking area, where our driver will retrieve them. God bless Veronica, who has contacted Drive Amalfi and asked them to pick up our bags at the usual spot but then to meet the two of us at a different location, so we won't have to walk up the back staircase where the steepest steps are. Instead, we will walk through town and up to the Mandara parking garage on Viale Pasitea. Grazie, Veronica.

As we get ready to check out of Hotel Pupetto and say our goodbyes, Gabriella asks Richard, "So will you come back, even with the steps?" Veronica smiles as she gives Richard a hug and asks him the same question.

"Well, we're not mountain goats, but yes, we'll be back," he says, laughing. "We've had a wonderful time here. Thank you for everything."

We meet Gabriella's mother as we head into town. She's pushing little Michele in a stroller, so we pause to say our goodbyes to them too. It doesn't take us long to reach the parking area meeting point. Funny how this walk seems easy after five days in Positano. The sun is shining and today is warm, definitely not a jacket kind of day, yet we are both wearing them to decrease the weight in our bags.

Since we have plenty of time, we find a bench not too far from the parking garage, and Richard waits for me while I walk across the street and check out the women's clothing shop of Maria Lampo. Inside, I find a nice variety of handmade linen clothes in bright colors. The pleasant women are friendly and helpful as I admire the fashions, although I decide to buy only a hat as a souvenir from Positano.

While I'm paying for my purchase, I learn that the three ladies inside are family members of the original owner, Maria. She opened this shop shortly after World War II, initially to make trousers for the sailors who lived here. I have the pleasure of meeting her beautiful daughter, Concetta Di Gennaro, and her two granddaughters, Emilia E. Graziano and Maria Esposito. Maria Lampo's shop is one of the original shops in Positano, and until recently, Maria was always here to greet her customers. Sadly, she passed away this past winter, and her granddaughter tells me how much they miss her. The people of Positano are so friendly, and this is just another example of how they make me feel like family. I say goodbye and will definitely be back.

Exactly on time, Biagio arrives in a Drive Amalfi Mercedes, and within minutes we are on our way to the airport. Traffic is almost nonexistent at this hour of the morning, and we enjoy a conversation with him about Italian politics and Italy's economic situation. He explains that he is from Furore, an Amalfi Coast town with only seven hundred people, and tells us he has been working on this coast as a driver for thirty years. As we pass Vesuvius, we can see it a little more clearly today, but the summit is still concealed by clouds.

In an hour and fifteen minutes, we arrive at Naples International Airport, and Biagio recommends a good place inside to have an authentic Neapolitan pizza. Since our Volotea flight isn't scheduled to leave until 2:45 p.m., we have time for a leisurely lunch. Fratelli la Bufala is our lunchtime destination and is not difficult to find, close to the arrivals area of the airport. Owned by three Italian brothers, this restaurant is modern, clean, and the *pizzaiolo* is in full view, making pizzas in the round, wood-burning oven. Richard and I split a margherita pizza, which costs €6.50, and the total bill, including a bottle of water and the *coperto*, is €12.50, very inexpensive for an airport meal. And although our only stops in Napoli this trip are at the train station and this airport, at least we are able to treat ourselves to a margherita pizza in Naples. I don't even need to tell you that the pizza is delicious.

***

We've been touring more than three weeks together in Europe now, and I'm loving traveling with Richard. After this amount of time we're starting to miss the little conveniences of home, like a clothes dryer and a large shower. But I wouldn't trade what we've experienced together. Being here with Richard helps me relax, and I find the time spent doing nothing makes me smile. I'm glad for once to have no agenda. It's new for me, but really good. No distractions, no worries about what I have to do, who I have to call, and best of all, what I have to check or post on social media, since I'm not working on this trip.

As we walk to our gate in the Naples airport, past the numerous duty-free shops and other Italian stores, we walk by Vincenzo Bellavia Pasticceria, and I see a *biscotto all'amarena*, a favorite of mine found only in Naples. I get excited and attract Richard's attention. "Oh my God, look what's here! *Amarena* biscotti!" Richard buys it for me. We share yet another thing from Italy.

***

I'll always miss my Amalfi Coast, especially Positano, but now I have unforgettable memories of sharing this special place with someone I love. My Amalfi Coast love affair encompasses much more meaning than it ever has before. Traveling to the Amalfi Coast alone or with friends has always been a highlight in Italy for me, and now, experiencing my favorite place in Italy with Richard is priceless.

About the Author

An award-winning author, Margie Miklas is a travel blogger, photographer, retired critical-care nurse, and social media manager. Her passion for travel embraces a particular love of Italy. When she's not writing, she enjoys traveling to Italy, spending time with her family, and relaxing at the beach. She makes her home in Florida and is a member of the Florida Writers Association.

Visit Margie at her blog, Margie in Italy

Margieinitaly.com

Thank you for reading *My Amalfi Coast Love Affair*. If you have the inclination, please consider writing a review for the author on Amazon.com, Goodreads and Barnes and Noble. It really does make a difference.

Also by Margie Miklas

Memoirs of a Solo Traveler – My Love Affair with Italy

My Love Affair with Sicily

Colors of Naples and the Amalfi Coast

Critical Cover-Up

Made in the USA
San Bernardino, CA
18 October 2018